THE Holy Spirit
Within

THE Holy Spirit
Within

HOMILIES AT ASCENSION AND PENTECOST

ST. JOHN OF AVILA

Scepter

NIHIL OBSTAT:
Andreas Moore, L.C.L. *Censor Duputatus*
IMPRIMATUR:
✠ Bishop E. Morrogh Bernard, *Vicar General*

The *Nihil Obstat* and *Imprimatur* are official declarations that these books are free of doctrinal or moral error. There are no implications contained therein that those who have granted the *Nihil Obstat* and *Imprimatur* agree with the content, opinion, or statements expressed.

First published in 1959 as *The Holy Ghost* by Scepter Publishers, Inc.

Scripture quotations in this book are from the Douay-Rheims

Translated by Ena Dargan

Copyright © 2012, Scepter Publishers, Inc.
PO Box 1391
New Rochelle, NY 10802
www.scepterpublishers.org

Text and cover design: Rose Design

Printed in the United States of America

ISBN: 978-1-59417-180-2

CONTENTS

INTRODUCTION

These six sermons on the Holy Spirit by St. John of Avila, like all his others which have survived, were taken down by his disciples as he delivered them. Usually he himself re-read and perfected them afterwards. Some of them are no more than a detailed outline of the sermon. But this does not mean that they have lost any of their original force, that force which, in the sixteenth century, provoked an outburst of fervor and devotion throughout the south of Spain. All St. John's sermons are of a very simple pattern. They begin with a short introduction, and then come to the central point. This is usually a single idea around which the famous preacher groups an abundance of texts from Holy Scripture, quotations from the Fathers, and well-chosen illustrations; all the time his own brilliant and original thought gives life to the particular truth which he wishes to impress on his hearers. The point of the sermon really comes to life. Then we find those dialogues, so typical of St. John, between the preacher and the souls of his astonished hearers—those of our own day as well as those of his—who find their difficulties and even their possible criticisms answered before they have had time to formulate them. Shocked with surprise, they feel reassured and, as it were, protected by the eternal truth which has been imparted to them.

The six sermons included in this volume are not the only ones, nor even perhaps the most significant, of St. John of Avila. But they deal with one of the most important subjects in the whole of his doctrine: the need for all the faithful—lay people as well as religious and priests—to know the Holy Spirit, to be in contact with Him and to surrender themselves to His impulses. It is He who completes the work of Jesus Christ in the souls of men: *si quis non habet Spiritum Christi, hic non est eius* (Rom 8:9). This, fundamentally, means reaffirming the need for a higher degree of mysticism—which consists essentially in the increasingly deeper and more constant operation of the Holy Spirit in the soul—in the perfection of life to which all Christians have been called. This doctrine, accepted by the whole Christian tradition up to the seventeenth century, has now begun to reclaim its due place after three centuries of neglect.

The dramatic value of St. John's oratorical style, the present-day importance of the doctrine contained in these sermons on the Holy Spirit, together with the simplicity and the spontaneity with which he treats of divine things make of these discourses a source of supernatural joy and a never-ending source of instruction "of great profit," as St. Teresa of Avila wrote in one of her letters.

Sermon I

∎ ∎ ∎

I have chosen no text for this sermon, because our text is nothing more than that we should prepare ourselves to be the dwelling place of the Holy Spirit, and that we should ask the Holy Spirit with great fervor to condescend to come to us. To ask Him, that is our only text. And we shall have accomplished not a little if we prepare ourselves, as we ought, to receive such a guest.

You know, of course, my brethren, that although the feasts of God are past events as far as history is concerned, the effects of these feasts are still with us. The time when Jesus Christ suffered is over. How unfortunate for us if the effects of His sufferings were over also. What would happen to us if the effects of the Passion, which took place over 1,000 years ago, were not to last? But they will persist to the end of the world. And although the feast of the Holy Spirit took place for the first time many years ago, you must bear in mind that the coming of the Holy Spirit will have exactly the same effect on your soul today, as it would have had in the time of the apostles: take care that you receive Him well.

Oh, who would not wish to have seen Jesus Christ when He was on earth suffering such hardships and to

1

have been able to ask favors of Him! If when He was in the world you could have thrown yourself at His feet, you feel certain that by virtue of His mercy and His infinite charity He would not have refused your requests. Do you believe this, brethren? Believe then that He is as ready and as willing to grant you those favors today though He is in heaven as ever He was when He lived amongst us on earth. And if at this time in your preparation for the coming of the Holy Spirit, you do everything that is necessary, I tell you on His behalf that the Holy Spirit will come to you bringing grace, just as He did to the apostles while they were living in the world.

What a holy time this is from now to the feast of Pentecost! A holy week indeed: the Advent of the Holy Spirit. The time after Our Lord's Ascension when the apostles were waiting for the fulfilment of the promise He had given them when He said to them: "I go . . . and I will ask the Father; and he shall give you another Paraclete," that is, comforter.[1] I shall send you the Paraclete who will console you for the sorrow that you will feel when I leave you. As they listened to these words, their eyes fixed on the sky, they waited to see what would happen. "Our Master," they said, "told us he would send us one to console us who will make us *forget* the love we feel for Him." The apostles were deeply attached to Our Lord and Savior. He was their consolation in sorrow, their Father in time of need, their teacher, a mirror in which they saw themselves. They depended on Him utterly. They were one with their Master. "That one shall come great enough, powerful enough, wise enough to make us forget our Master. Who can this be?" Raising their thoughts and their voices to heaven, they said: "Lord, we long for Thee and we do not know Thee; we wish Thee to come and we do not know who Thou art. Of thy mercy, deign to come and console our hearts; come Lord for we are indeed sorrowful without Thee."

Such was the attitude of the holy apostles of the Lord at that holy time; and we would do well to imitate them, since we are one with them, one church and one in union with Jesus Christ. All those who serve Jesus Christ are one, belong to the church of God and the Christian congregation. *Una est amica mea, una est columba mea.* God speaks to His church and says: "Thou art one, my love; thou art one, my dove."[2] And so it is right also that in this holy season we should prepare ourselves, and with the holy apostles desire the coming of the Holy Spirit. Let us raise our hearts to heaven and, our eyes full of tears, let us cry: "Comforter of my soul! Come, console me!" And during all this time let us do nothing else but desire the Holy Spirit to come to our souls.[3]

The *first* requirement for the coming of the Holy Spirit to our souls is that we should be aware of His power, and that we should believe that He can accomplish marvels. However sad a soul may be, He is sufficient to console it; however worthless, He can make it valuable; however lukewarm, He can fire it; however weak, He can strengthen it; however lacking in piety, He can inflame it with ardent devotion. What is the way to bring the Holy Spirit to us? It is to be aware of His might. And it has been said of the might of the Holy Spirit: "For, great is the power of God alone: and he is honored by the humble."[4]

The *second* requirement for the Holy Spirit to be willing to come into our hearts (so that we may not be rejected or found wanting) is to have the will to receive Him as our guest, sincerely and anxiously to desire His coming. "Oh, if only the Holy Spirit would come! Oh, if that Comforter would only visit me and console my soul!"

Know, my brethren, that attending to our bodily needs will greatly impede the Holy Spirit coming to us. Here religious are at an advantage; because whether they are in the choir, or in the refectory, or in their cells, they are always engaged in the business of looking after their souls, always praising Jesus Christ; always thanking Him. And whether they are eating or drinking or engaged in any human activity it is for the sole purpose of praising God.[5]

Married persons are indeed daring. The married woman may think that on rising she has no duty other than to take her cloak, go off to hear a sermon and get herself a good place in the church. Then when her husband comes to his meal and finds it has not yet been cooked, he loses his temper and offends God. It would be better, my sister, if before you went out, you had left your house in order, and when everything was in readiness, you could come to the sermon. If you arrive a little late it does not matter, one word may well be of more profit to you than the whole sermon. Of course you could perform all these duties, but since you seem unable to do so, it would be better for you to devote yourself entirely to the obligations of the married state.

Those who marry are indeed daring, for they take on grave responsibilities. They must maintain a household, support their children and bring them up to be virtuous; and the wife must train them and teach them to behave themselves as they should. But this is by no means all. What of the care of one's soul and of one's work in the service of God? All these duties can be accomplished: but the things of the world are alluring and it is difficult to free oneself from them. For this reason it is not easy for the married man with many responsibilities to be able to attend to his soul as he ought. Take care, my brother, how you live! Take care that you do not come to love your wife so much that in order to give her a present you will offend God as Adam did! "I love my wife very much. I must give her this jewel and although I know I am doing what I ought not to do, I will give it to her all the same." And you, wife, do not love your husband so much that you will come to forget God, forget to carry out your religious duties, and forget the law of God!

Oh, what care those who are going to be married should take before their marriage! How holy the man and the woman should be! Before they come together they should have spent many years in the service of God; they should have learnt to be chaste, to be humble, to be patient, to be merciful, to keep the commandments of Our Lord. Only then should they get married so that although later on they may have many worries and many upsets and obstacles, one glance at their former way of life and they will have a pattern of behavior to fall back on and will be at peace. Like a master who has a servant so well trained and so afraid of him, that he has only to look at him and the servant will get ready to serve him.

But if the married man does not know what marriage means and even less the married woman: they come together and later their marriage becomes defiled.

There are many lessons to be learnt. "How, Father, how can I look after my household and serve God at the same time?" It is very difficult. St. Paul says: "But he that is with a wife"—he that is married—"is solicitous for the things of the world; how he may please his wife. And he is divided. And the unmarried woman and the virgin thinketh on the things of the Lord; that she may be holy both in body and in spirit."[6]

Brethren, this feast will be spent in thinking how I may please my Lord. Like brides who are careful to have their hair perfectly groomed, to have their clothes neat, and who even carry a mirror about with them in case they should become disarranged, so should the reverend mothers, the nuns and novices be particular not to wear a garment that is indecorous: they must look at themselves in Jesus Christ as in a mirror to see there is neither a spot on their garments, nor any sin or stain on their soul lest their spouse should reject them.

Be devoted and faithful in the service of Jesus Christ and in your hopes for the coming of the Holy Spirit, and have no dealings with evil and meanness, because the consolation of the Spirit is very gentle. Very little will hinder its coming and it does not take pleasure in the things of this world. St. Bernard says: "The Divine consolation is gentle and exacting, and it is not given to those who accept human consolation."[7] Let every soul rid itself of human consolation if it wishes the Holy Spirit to console it and wishes His consolation to remain always with it. For, as we said, it is right and proper that the Holy Spirit should wish to be desired.

Listen carefully to me! If a man will not go to another man's house because he is not sure of his welcome there, will this not also be the attitude of the Holy Spirit? He wants the man who desires His presence to desire it greatly; and He wishes to be desired by many. How the coming of Our Savior was desired! Adam, Noah, Abraham, Isaac, Jacob, the prophets and patriarchs all longed for His coming. "Drop down dew, ye heavens, from above: and let the clouds rain the just. Let the earth be opened and bud forth a savior."[8] The prophet Haggai said: "For thus saith the Lord of hosts: Yet one little while, and I will move the heaven and the earth and the sea and the dry land. And I will move all nations: and the desired of all nations shall come.[9] And the angel of the testament whom you desire shall come to his temple."[10] The coming of Jesus Christ was greatly desired and the Holy Spirit wishes to be desired. For it is fitting that the gift of the Holy Spirit should be ardently desired before we receive it. The dish that is good of itself is wasted on him who has no wish for food. You would imagine that a chicken or a partridge would give anyone an appetite. But the sick man to whom it is offered says "Take it away, for I have lost all interest in food! I have no taste for it." A very bad sign indeed. You have no interest in food? It is a symptom of death.

The Holy Spirit will not come to you if you do not hunger for Him, if you do not desire Him. Your desires for God will bring God to you, and the proof is that if you desire God He will come to you without delay. Do not tire of longing for His presence and although you wait for Him and He does not come, and although you call Him and He does not answer, persevere in your desire and He will not fail you. Brethren have confidence in Him, even if He does not come immediately when you call. He will come when He sees that you have fulfilled the necessary conditions. You must, brethren, compose your hearts because if you are distressed and call on the Holy Spirit and He does not come, it is because you have not yet the right dispositions. And if He does not come, it is not because He does not want to come, nor that He has forgotten you, but so that you may persevere in your desire for Him. By thus persevering you will make yourself fit to receive Him, you will be able to make room for Him in your heart, and increase your trust in him. I promise you on His behalf that nobody who calls on Him will be left without His consolation.

As the royal prophet David says: "He hath not slighted nor despised the supplication of the poor man."[11] Who is poor? He is poor who mistrusts himself and relies only on God: he is poor who mistrusts his own opinions and strength, his own gifts, his own powers; he is poor who knows his own vileness, his own littleness; who knows he is a worm and full of corruption, and with all this relies only on God for protection and believes that God's mercy is so great that He will not leave him without His consolation. "The desires of such as these are heard by God."

And observe that merely to harbor these desires is not enough to content the Holy Spirit. You have not yet done enough, my brethren, there must be in addition action. Do you want a proof? Note what was said to the apostles, when they were looking up at the sky in suspense, when the Lord ascended into heaven. They were closely united to Him. They were longing and hoping for the visit of the Holy Spirit; they were anxious to see the Holy Spirit as their Master had declared they would; they were oblivious of themselves, as they looked at Jesus Christ when He ascended into heaven. Blessed be He, who was so solicitous for our good; who did not content Himself merely with looking after us and taking care of us; but when He had ascended into heaven was so anxious about His own, that He sent down two angels dressed in white garments who said to them: "Ye men of Galilee, why stand you looking up to heaven? This Jesus who is taken up from you into heaven shall so come—with the same majesty—as you have seen him going into heaven."[12] And they were told to go to the Cenacle, because there the Holy Spirit would come upon them. You need not spend the whole day looking into the sky; you need not spend it praying or meditating. Go, my brethren, to the Cenacle. Do not spend your time thinking on the bodily presence of Christ!

I have often said to you that the reason the Holy Spirit did not come to the apostles while Jesus Christ was in this world was because they were transported in the Master's presence, and that alone contented them, and although the presence of Our Lord was so good and holy, it hindered the apostles from being perfect, and on this account Jesus Christ wished to go away. "My disciples, you are deeply attached to Me, you love Me greatly. I know that when you are with Me you are content; but I love you even more and to prove My love, I shall go away, so that the Holy Spirit may come and make you more perfect, and bring your thoughts closer to God." Does this not show you that the presence of Jesus Christ in some degree hindered the coming of the Holy Spirit?

The Holy Spirit is indeed jealous. Do not think He is not exacting. "I am the Lord,"[13] said God to Moses. So that you may understand, brethren, that if you are fond of your confessor, however holy he may be, or of the preacher who gives you good advice and consoles you, the Holy Spirit will not come until you have renounced an excessive love of human beings. The Holy Spirit wishes to be alone with you.

"But, Father, he is a saint, and guides me along the road to God, and encourages me when I am in difficulties." Jesus Christ was holier and even He hindered the coming of the Holy Spirit. The servant of God, the confessor and the preacher should not stand in the way of the Holy Spirit, who should be a staircase up which you can climb to God. Love—even innocent love—will stand in the way. Love would not do you any harm if you knew how to enjoy it properly. What you love in the confessor and the preacher let it be for God and in God. "How shall I know, Father, when this love is in God?" If you like someone very much, and God takes him from you, or separates you from him, and you continue unperturbed in the service of God, the love is in God. I mean that if the parting does not cause you to be upset, overwhelmed, and neglectful of your duties, in that case the love is in God. A little suffering is natural, but a lot of suffering is not good. If motes like these hinder the coming of the Holy Spirit, what will be the effect of evil thoughts, violent language, and the like?

What is the position? What is necessary so that the Holy Spirit may come to our souls? Not only must we desire Him, but we must get ready our house and have it spotless for Him. You do as much when you are expecting a guest. But since the guest that you are awaiting is infinitely pure, how much more necessary that your soul should be unspotted, that your thoughts, your words, your deeds should be free from evil and that you should be adorned with all the virtues.

Besides being necessary to call upon the Holy Spirit and to prepare the dwelling, it is essential to get ready the repast. Put your hand into your pocket, and do not regret having to spend freely. You must be open-handed and liberal! When you have a guest, not only do you not grudge buying sufficient for his entertainment but you will provide more than sufficient. That, brethren, is how we should get ready for this most holy guest; since He is so open-handed with you, be you the same with Him; put your hand into your pocket and do not give ungenerously! Give charity in abundance; feed the hungry, dress the orphan and the widow, be a father to those in trouble! Be a father to the poor! Holy Job performed this duty as we know from his own words. Lord, "if I have eaten my morsel alone . . ."[14] And elsewhere: "I was an eye to the blind, and a foot to the lame."[15]

Give the Holy Spirit to eat, and give Him your heart: He eats flesh; but see that it is mortified flesh. How would it be if you gave your guest a live bird? "What is this?"—he would say to you—"Take it away. That bird is not fit to eat."

Raise your heart often to heaven and beg that it may be fired with love. Your flesh must be dead and some time dead, punished and mortified, subjugated with fasts and scourgings; it must be dead to the world. Guard your heart carefully! Raise your thoughts and desires to God! Become as a golden eagle through these thoughts and exercises: soar upwards and do not rest until you have reached the Holy Spirit: do not relax your efforts or let your mind dwell on things that are corrupt or ignoble. Remember what the dove did when it was let loose from Noah's Ark. By the time it left the Ark, the flood had ceased. It flew about but did not alight upon any of the dead bodies or even go near them. It flew to an olive tree, broke off a twig with its beak and returned with it to the Ark. This is what the Christian soul should do—not be preoccupied with corruption. Do not let your thoughts dwell on things corrupt or perishable or noisome, but on heaven. "Where thy treasure is, there is thy heart"[16] and more especially during this season.

Seek seclusion throughout this week in preparation for the Holy Spirit! Be on your guard! Remember those servants who were waiting for their master to come from the wedding.[17] Do not be like those foolish and stupid virgins; do not be imprudent; do not be intoxicated by the things of this world. Imitate the wise virgins in their prudence and preparation; and, obtaining the oil of mercy for yourself first of all in attending to the needs of your soul, try to become more holy in heart. During these days find a secluded corner for yourself and stay there. Contemplate the Blessed Virgin and the holy apostles gathered together in the Cenacle. How would they have behaved?

What would they do? How they would have wept thinking of the passion of Jesus Christ, sorrowful for His absence. What sighs they would send to heaven, longing for this Holy Spirit their comforter and their healer. Temper your desires, mortify and lower your eyes, look at nothing you would regret seeing; because if the eye sees, the eye will weep. David saw an evil sight—it would have been better for him to be blind than to have seen what he saw; for if his eyes delighted in looking at that sight, they wept later; wept so much that David, they say, had furrows in his cheeks worn by his tears.

And it is essential to observe great reverence during this week, since we are preparing for such a great feast. Do you know brethren, how important is this occasion and what you will lose if the Holy Spirit does not come to dwell in your house? For neither the feast of the Incarnation of Jesus Christ—the principal feast of the whole year—nor the feasts of His holy birth, passion, or redemption and ascension into heaven will benefit your soul if you do not profit by this feast; and all that Jesus Christ gained for us will be lost to you. Although it is true that with the death of Jesus Christ heaven was opened and hell shut—how can this benefit you, if you do not receive the Holy Spirit? Without the grace of God nothing can help you. But if the Holy Spirit is within you, you can avail yourself of all those other aids and consolations.

The Holy Spirit is sufficient to console you and strengthen your weakness and bring you happiness. He has indeed the power to do so. I knew of one to whom the Holy Spirit came in small measure and he went shouting through the streets like a madman. Do you want proof? Look at the apostles: before the Holy Spirit came down on them they were so timid and so faint-hearted that they did not dare to go out, but kept the door of their house shut. After the Holy Spirit had come upon them they opened wide the doors, and went out into the streets and began to preach in the name of Jesus Christ.

St. Athanasius—the great saint who wrote against the Arian heresy—describing the scruples from which some people suffer as to whether they possessed the Holy Spirit within them—"Am I baptized or not?" The reply to them: "Do you know how you will be sure? As the pregnant woman feels the child stir within her, so will you feel the movement of the Holy Spirit." "But Father, I am a man and not a married woman. I do not know what the movement of a child would feel like. How shall I feel the Holy Spirit?" "I give you this sign, my brethren. You will feel your heart burning with the fire of charity and the unwavering love of God (because the Holy Spirit is fire) and you will feel this flame of love leaping within you." "How can this be, Father?"[18] Christ Himself gives the answer in his conversation with the Samaritan woman: "He that shall drink of the water that I will give him . . ." "What is this water like, Lord?" "It shall become in him a fountain of water, springing up into life everlasting."[19] This is the sign given by Christ by which we can recognize the coming to us of the Holy Spirit. For the Holy Spirit has this quality. His presence cannot be concealed, and the Holy Spirit Himself told us how we can know with certainty that Jesus Christ has come to us. Christ says in the Gospel which is read in the Mass: "When the Paraclete comes, when the Holy Spirit comes, the Spirit of Truth "whom the Father will send in my name, he will teach you all things and bring all things to your mind, whatsoever I shall have said to you."[20] Which means that He will console you, enlighten you, refresh you, and direct you.

The Holy Spirit is the Comforter, brethren. The Holy Spirit can indeed console, since in His greatness He is called *Comforter.* What do we want in this life? What are we seeking here below? We spend our lives striving to achieve a small measure of happiness. Then why not strive to have within us a Comforter who will console us and will enrich our souls? Oh if I could only inspire you with devotion to the Holy Spirit! May He through His infinite mercy do so!

When you are sad, you may be certain that if He is within you, the Holy Spirit will console you. St. Paul the apostle, says: Because if any man ask himself "Who will suffice to console my sadness, who will remove my fear?" If there are "combats without, fears within," let him remember that "God who comforteth the humble comforted us."[21]

The function of the Holy Spirit is to comfort those who are sorrowful. It has been proclaimed and published throughout the whole church of Jesus Christ Our Lord that He is our Comforter in affliction. A sick man will get a doctor to cure him. He who wants to go to law will get a good advocate to plead for him. He will approach the judge and say "Give a verdict in my favor." We are all sad. We all need someone to whom we can turn for consolation. The wicked are sad, because of the evil they have committed.

Even the just find their sins weighing heavily upon them, and if they offend God and lose Him, they are plunged in grief. We are all sad. And all of us need a comforter. It is the function of the Holy Spirit to console all who are in trouble. Let us ask Him to deign to come to our hearts and console us.

A soul which is intimidated and frightened because it has committed a great number of sins may well say: "Father, this Holy Spirit, who you say is God, is an all-powerful, a terrifying God: I am a worm, an ant: how could the Holy Spirit be willing to come to me, whose dwelling place is so unprepared? I fear He would not want to come."

If you are only thinking of your own unworthiness, you are quite right. But do you know the solution? Place Jesus Christ as a mediator between you and Him; and the Holy Spirit seeing what Jesus Christ suffered for you, will come for love of Him. Since there is One who suffered unhappiness, so that you might be consoled, was sad that you might be happy, fatigued that you might rest, died that you might live, you have no cause for fear, if you are truly sorry for your sins and do penance for them. Blessed be Jesus Christ and may his angels bless Him! Amen!

Our Redeemer said: "And I looked for one that would grieve together with me, but there was none: and for one that would comfort me, and I found none. And they gave me gall for my food: and in my thirst they gave me vinegar to drink."[22] Our Redeemer found none to console Him; He was grief-stricken, disconsolate and could find no comfort; He was overwhelmed with sorrow from within and without that He said *Tristis est anima mea usque ad mortem,*[23] which means that Our Redeemer was sorrowful unto death. We do not refer to the divine aspect of His soul which enjoyed God from eternity; but to its sensitivity. This made Him sad in the extreme. What weariness he suffered! How He hungered and thirsted and sweated while He was in the world! And when the time for suffering came He was so distressed at the thought of it that He said "If this chalice may not pass away, but I must drink it, thy will be done."[24] In the indescribable sufferings which He underwent, Christ Our Redeemer also said, in His weakness as man, *Deus meus, Deus meus, ut quid dereliquisti me?*[25] So much, brethren, did Our Lord undergo, so great was His suffering, His scourging, His crowning with thorns, the blows which He received in His sacred face, that He Himself said: O *vos omnes, qui transitis per viam;* "O all ye that pass by the way," all who live in the world, "attend, and see if there be any sorrow like to my sorrow."[26] Blessed be Thou, my Redeemer, for ever!

Why didst Thou suffer such agony, Lord? Are not suffering and torments the penalty for sin, the punishment of the wicked?

Those who sin deserve punishment. But Thou, Lord, what wrong didst Thou do that Thou shouldst suffer so much? Why didst Thou undergo such agony?

Our Redeemer Jesus Christ said: "What debt do these men owe?" "Lord, they have committed many sins." "Well, then," said Jesus Christ "I want their punishment to fall on Me, so that the peace of heaven may come down on them. I want to suffer affliction and grief, so that happiness may come to them. I wish to be given gall, so that they may receive honey, to suffer so that they may have peace, to die that they may have life."

Have confidence in the merits of Jesus Christ. Do not think that no voice is raised to defend you in heaven; the merits of Jesus Christ are there, pleading for you. Nor is He silent if you are begging the Holy Spirit to come to you. Do not doubt but that if you offer up the merits of Jesus Christ you will, through them, receive the Holy Spirit. Your offering is of equal value as what you obtain. If you receive God, you also give God, and although Jesus Christ, Our Redeemer, did not suffer in His divinity, nevertheless He *did* suffer and He *is* God. And in exchange for the gall which He drank when He hung on the cross, you will receive the honey of the Holy Spirit.

Your thoughts, words, and deeds will call out to the Holy Spirit, and He will come over you, without your knowing how, nor in what way, without your being aware how He entered your soul. You will find Him dwelling in your heart; you will feel within your soul a great happiness, a joy so wonderful, so all-pervading that you will be transported. Holy King David said "To my hearing thou shalt give joy and gladness: and the bones that have been humbled shall rejoice."[27] The heart that was sad, the soul that was cast down, will be glad and rejoice. You will hear the Holy Spirit speaking to you and advising you what you must do.

And as His function is to console you, it is also to exhort you. In the same way as He comforts you, so will He admonish you. "O cowardly and fainthearted creature that you are, do not be timid like a child! Have the courage of a man!" The same Holy Spirit who comes to console you, will also warn you so that you may rid yourself of everything that might prevent His consolation reaching you. *Paracletus* means Comforter.

Since then, through the merits of Jesus Christ, the Holy Spirit gives Himself to us, do not cease to ask for Him and to desire Him ardently! Dedicate yourself to Him who will come to your soul and you will receive great consolation and no one will succeed in taking Him from you. Prepare your dwelling place! Prepare the food for this Guest! He deserves all you do for Him, and you are under so many obligations to Him. Let us give generously to the poor; let us perform works of mercy among our neighbors; let us abstain from all sin and from all imperfections in this holy week; let our senses be subjugated and let us all have complete confidence that He through His mercy will come to us in flames of love, to fortify us and bring us His gifts.

Notes

1. Jn 14:2, 16.
2. Song 6:8.
3. Mass of Pentecost Sunday, seq.
4. Eccl 3:21.
5. 1 Cor 10:31.
6. 1 Cor 7:33.
7. The idea occurs frequently in the writings of St. Bernard. Cf. *In Vigilia Nativ. Domini. Serm.* 4, 1. *In Ps. Qui habitat serm.* 9, 6; in *Ascens. Domini. Serm.* 3, 7; serm. 5, 9ff: ML 183, 100, 219, 307, 319ff.

8. Cf. Is 45:8.

9. Hg 2:7–8.

10. Cf. Mal 3:1.

11. Cf. Ps 21:25.

12. Cf. Acts 1:11.

13. E. 20:2; cf. 34:14.

14. Jb 31:17.

15. Jb 29:15.

16. Mt 6:21; cf. Mt 25:2ff.

17. Lk 12:36.

18. St. Athanasius, *De Trinitage et Spiritu Sancto*, 20. MG 25, 1215; Ep. 3, ad Serap., 3; MG 24, 627ff.

19. Cf. Jn 4:13–14.

20. Jn 14:26

21. 2 Cor 8:5–6.

22. Ps 68:21–22.

23. Mt 26:38.

24. Mt 26:42.

25. Mt 27:46.

26. Lam 1:12.

27. Ps 50:10.

Sermon II

Cum venerit Paracletus, quem ego mittam vibos a Patre,
Spiritum veritatis, qui a Patre procedit, ille testimonium
perhibebit de me (John 15:26).

■ ■ ■

Omnes quaerunt quae sua sunt, non quae Jesu Christi,[1] says
St. Paul the Apostle, complaining of the ways of men. "For
all seek the things that are their own; not the things that
are Jesus Christ's." And speaking of Jesus Christ he says:
Etenim Christus non sibi placuit, sed sic (ut) scriptum est,
improperia improperantium tibi ceciderunt super me.[2] All
seek the things that are their own, but not those concerned
with Jesus Christ; but Christ was forgetful of His own good
so that He might be mindful of ours. *Non sibi placuit.* He
did not choose a pleasant life in the material sense. On the
contrary He was often tired as He went about on earth; He
wept copiously, suffered death, so that man might understand that though He could have lived a life free from care,
He renounced tranquility so that men might enjoy it.

Lord! If Thou were like us, how terrible it would be!
How often has it happened that you have gone to Our Lord
to ask Him for some favor, pestering Him with prayers,
alms, tears, and mortifications and after He has granted it,

21

you, like a bad debtor, forget all about God? You go to the Lord in adversity, and in prosperity you forget Him. That is bad. If He were like us, what would become of us? Now He is in Heaven, He is no longer in need of our help. If He forgot us in prosperity, what would become of us? Blessed be His mercy! Jesus Christ entered into heaven itself, says St. Paul, that he might appear in the presence of God to offer His passion and obtain the Holy Spirit for us.[3]

We will be helped through the intercession of Jesus Christ because we will receive the Holy Spirit. Mary, will we be helped through your intercession? Rachel had two children; the most blessed Virgin has two children! One the child of her body, the other an adopted child. Her own child is now reigning in heaven, where nothing can harm Him; there is no longer need to ask favors for Him. But she may obtain for us her adopted children the grace to help us do right, never to speak evil, and the grace of a happy death. We ask her to do this for us when we pray to her: Hail Mary . . .

When the Paraclete cometh. This is Pentecost week. May the Holy Spirit come into your hearts, so that you may have a holy Pentecost.

Jesus Christ says in St. John, Chapter 15: "When the Paraclete cometh, whom I will send you from the Father, the Spirit of truth, who proceedeth from the Father, he shall give testimony of me. And you shall give testimony"—because you have been eye-witnesses, "because you are with me from the beginning."[4] Prepare yourselves, for disasters shall overtake you; "they will put you out of the synagogues" and will persecute you, and the one consoling thought which you might have is that one day they will cease to persecute you. But even this you cannot hope for. They will never stop persecuting you because "who soever killeth you, will think he doth a service to God." You can console yourselves by remembering that they are ignorant: "They have not known the Father nor me," and they persecute you, though you do not deserve persecution, for love of Me. "But these things I have told you that when the hour shall come, you may remember that I told you" of the good and evil "that will come to you," and "you will know that I tell you the truth."[5] This is a quotation from the gospel. It is indeed concise.

When the Paraclete cometh. I have said to you several times that if we allow the Lord to do with us as His Heart desires, He will bestow His mercy upon us, because *it is His nature to bestow mercy;* if He chastises us, it is because He is obliged to, but to do so is against His wishes. *Non enim humiliavit ex corde quo, et abiecit filios hominum.*[6] When God humbles a man, He does not do it willingly, but because He is forced to. He is like a father who see-ing his child doing wrong, punishes him though he loves him, because the child has obliged him to do so. "God, by nature, is gentle" —says St. Jerome— "but we force Him to chastise us."[7] For this reason, when He punishes, He seeks consolation. *Quondam si abiecit, et miserebit (ur) secundum multitudinem misericordiarum suarum.*[8]

How sorrowful the apostles became when He told them that He was leaving them. *Quia haec dixi vobis, tristitia implevit cor vestrum.*[9] They loved Jesus Christ so much that they could not bear to hear Him say "I am going away." Since Thou art so ready to give comfort, what consolation wilt Thou give these men who are so sad for love of Thee?

He makes two statements to them by way of consolation. *Si diligeretis me, gauderetis utique.*[10] Do not subordinate My happiness in favor of your own pleasure. If you loved Me, you would indeed rejoice, because I am going to reign in heaven. The comfort He offered them was a counsel of perfection; by way of giving them further consolation He told them that the life of suffering which lay before them was God's will for them and that His departure would be to their advantage. "Sorrow hath filled your heart" because I go. "But I tell you the truth; it is expedient to you that I go." Mark that saying; for great faith is needed to believe it: "I tell you the truth; it is expedient to you that I go." Do you imagine that you will remain defenseless because I am leaving, and the Jews and all men will persecute you? Are you like children who think they will be eaten by the wolf, once they are separated from their mother?

Lord, if You told us that this parting would benefit You we could understand; but that it will benefit us, how is that possible? *Si enim non abiero, Paracletus non veniet ad vos.* "It is expedient to you that I go. For if I go not, the Paraclete will not come to you; but if I go, I will send him to you."[11] That is why it will be to your advantage if I leave. Lord! One Paraclete in exchange for another? Dolt Thou not comfort us?

Did not the Lord speak well of this Paraclete so that His coming might lessen the pain of His own departure?

"I shall send you one whose name is Paraclete, one who will teach you not only about the things of today, but even about the things of the future; who will tell you who I am, for you do not yet know Me well; one who is the Spirit, who will make you understand in your inmost soul that it is not necessary to have ears to hear Him, or eyes to see Him; one who will never leave you but who will be with you when you eat, when you sleep, when you are in the church, and when you are at home; one who indeed will be your companion, for He will never be separated from you. Be glad that I am going, because this Teacher is coming to you. All that I have told you, He will expound. He will be your Master, your Tutor, your Comforter. He will console you. Be glad that I am going.

The Spirit is indeed great in dignity, for Jesus Christ Himself preached about Him. Who preached about Jesus Christ? The Holy Spirit Himself through the mouths of the prophets; but Jesus Christ Himself, God and Man, spoke about the Holy Spirit with His own lips and praised Him greatly so that the apostles might resign themselves to His departure.

"Lord, one Paraclete in exchange for another? Wilt Thou not remain? We are happy with Thee. There is no sorrow that Thy presence will not take away. Remain with us, Lord!" "You are wrong." The humanity of Jesus Christ, the Man, was not perfect as the Holy Spirit is perfect. For the humanity of Christ was created and the Holy Spirit was God. The divinity of Christ did not go away, because His divinity had not come down from heaven; neither did His divinity rise to heaven; only His body and soul left the world, and as Man, He was less than the Holy Spirit. You are wrong then to ask Him not to go. The Holy Spirit must come. "When the Paraclete cometh, he shall give testimony of me."[12] And when you know who I am, then you will understand that it is right that I should leave."

We have reached the point I wanted to come to. To each his particular pleasure. Mine is indeed far from lofty, but one of the times when my soul is happiest, and hopes to receive the greatest favors from God, is during this feast of Pentecost, indeed a most holy week. In courtesy to God, do me this favor, by which you will render service to God, and great good to your soul: this week serve God very faithfully even if you have not done so in the past, and I promise you on God's behalf, in whose place I stand, although unworthily, that He will repay you the service you render Him. He who takes part in this feast, takes part in all the other feasts of the year. He who does not take part in it, shares neither in Christ's birth nor in His fasts, nor His prayers, His scourging, His death, His resurrection, nor in His ascension. He who does not participate in this feast has no share in anything Christ has done or ever will do.

Do you think this is to esteem this feast too highly? Jesus did all that He did in order that men might take part in this feast. *Ut divinitatis suae tribueret nos esse participes.*[13] So sings the church at this time.—To participate in His divinity: what does that mean?—It means to celebrate this feast fittingly, to receive the Holy Spirit, who is God Himself. It was for this that Jesus Christ strove so hard: that we might benefit by this feast.—And what feast is this?—The feast of the Holy Spirit.—Can I not get on well enough without the Holy Spirit.—No, indeed. Woe to him who has not the

Holy Spirit within him.—Can I not live merely the life of the flesh, or at least of my own spirit?—No. St. Paul says: *Vos autem in came non estis, sed in spiritu. Si quis spiritum Christi non habet, hic non est ejus.* Let none be dismayed. You—says St. Paul—do not live in the flesh; you do not live by your own wisdom; your conduct is not ruled by your will, your own desires. He who was such a great preacher said to you in truth: "But you are not in the flesh, but in the spirit," *si tamen,* or *si quidem,* as he says elsewhere, *Spiritus Dei habitat in vobis;*[14] because the Spirit of God abides within you. And so that you may understand that your beatitude depends on having the Holy Spirit as your guest know that "if any man have not the Spirit of Christ, he is none of His." It is necessary to say this again and again. If he does not belong to Christ, to whom does he belong?

All my riches consist, Oh King, in belonging to Thee; and on this condition God gives riches to the Christian provided that he belongs to God: *Omnia vestra sunt; sive Paulus, sive Apollo, sive Cephas, sive mundus, sive vita, sive mors, sive praesentia, sive futura, omnia enim vestra sunt, vos autem Christi, Christus autem Dei.*[15] Do not consider yourselves poor, *for all things are yours: Paul is* yours, because he works and suffers for you. *Cephas,* which means Peter, is yours, because he too toils and exhausts himself as a slave in your service. *Apollo* also. This preacher is yours that preaches to *you. Life* is yours since you are living it for God; *death* is yours because through death you reach God; *the present* and *the future* are yours —the present because you are using it as God wills and the future is being kept for you. All things are yours and you are Christ's. All things are yours provided you are Christ's. If you were not Christ's, to whom would you belong? *Qui incredulus est Filio, non videbit vitam; sed ira Dei manes super eum.* "He that believeth not the Son of God," he who is out of favor with Him, "the wrath of God abideth on him."[16]

The wrath of God began with Adam, and we are all born children of wrath; Jesus Christ brought grace, and the wrath of God abideth on all who do not belong to Christ. Justice is in Jesus Christ. Sin is in Adam. Grace is in Jesus Christ. In Adam is hell. In Jesus Christ heaven. If you are not living in Christ, if He is not pleased with you, the wrath of God abideth on you. *In peccatores respicit ira illius.* "His wrath looketh upon sinners." [17] When man commits mortal sin he is dead to God, who looks upon him with anger. Who would hold back the hand of God? Who will defend you from Him? *Scapulis suds obumbravit tibi.*[18] —Who will save you from the wrath of God?—The gentleness of God.—Who will save you from a stern God?—The Lamb of God. God sent His son so that suffering and punishment should fall on Him, who owed nothing, and that the guilty should go free; because *He will overshadow you with his shoulders* and the wrath of God will not consume you. Place yourself behind Him so that the heat of the sun will reach Him, and the wrath of God fall on Him. Behind Him there is protection. Behind Him you will find refuge.

If I do not abide in Christ, what will happen to me? If the branch does not remain on the vine, it will be burnt.[19] And if you do not abide in Jesus Christ you will not escape hell. "No man hath ascended into heaven, but he that descended from heaven, the Son of man."[20] *No* one will enter into glory, save he who is pleasing to God, who is loved by the Father. And no one is pleasing to God if he be not in Jesus Christ. He who is not united to Jesus Christ will be condemned for eternity. "If any man have not the Spirit of Christ, he is none of His." Woe to that man!

Take from me, Lord, all that the sky and the earth contains, but do not prevent me belonging to You; Thy meekness will direct me; if I am not Thine, I will be ruled by wrath, lust, passion. Beware of being governed by such masters as these, for they are all passions. How could they guide you aright?

There are no harsher words than these: *Qui non habet Spiritum Christi, hic non est ejus. Conterriti sunt in Sion peccatores; possedit tremor hypocritas.*[21] It is imperative that today I should talk to your hearts, and make you witnesses against yourselves. "The sinners in Sion are afraid, trembling hath seized upon the hypocrites." Why? *Qui non habet Spiritum Christi, hic non est ejus.* These are harsh words. But you must not become dismayed so easily.

It is not enough that you live in the flesh, nor that you live the life of your own spirit. Do not think that it is sufficient simply to put your hand into your pocket and give alms: you must do it in the Spirit of God. God is Spirit and loves His like; he wants you to adore Him and serve Him in the spirit. If the spirit of charity is not within you, it will avail you nothing to give alms. What will it profit you to tell your beads over and over again if the spirit within you is not praying? *Populus hic labiis me honorat, cor autem eorum longe est a me.*[22] Or what use is the white surplice, which is the sign of chastity, if neither the spirit nor the body is

chaste? Or what use is it to bend your knees, if your soul is
unbending, and does not wish to humble itself and obey
God and His holy laws? It is necessary to serve Him in
mind and deed. Are you then to be content to serve God
with your body and with your spirit? No. Let no one be
dismayed, I will tell you when to get frightened.

"If any man hath not the spirit of Christ, he is none of
His." Your own spirit is not enough.—I do not understand.
I am satisfied with it. Is it not sufficient that a man should
live according to his reason and that his passions should
be restrained and controlled by his own will? No. St. John
says: *Dedit eis potestatem filios Dei fieri his qui credunt in
nomine ejus; qui non ex sanguinibus, neque ex voluntate
carnis, neque ex voluntate viri, sed ex Deo nati stunt.*[23] Oh
how well you have expressed it, Oh Eagle of God! Those
who are the children of God are born, not of men, "not of
blood, nor of the will of the flesh, nor of the will of man,
but of God." It is not enough to be born of blood if you
wish to be children of God and to go to heaven. It will not
help you at all to be the son of a count, or of a duke, or to
be of royal blood. That is not important. The greatest Seraphim in heaven, if he had not the spirit of Christ within
him, would not be beatified. Heaven is not given to those
of high birth, *non ex sanguinibus, neque ex voluntate carnis.*
They are not born of the will, that accedes to the desires
of the flesh, that is subjugated by the flesh. And he who is
born of the will ordered by reason, is a man; he who lives
according to the flesh does not deserve the name of man.
To possess heaven, it is not enough merely to be a man:
Quod enim natum est ex came, caro est.[24]

Nemo ascendit in caelum, nisi qui descendit de caelo, filius hominis.[25] To be a man you must abide in Christ so that you may ascend to heaven in Him. If you are nothing more than a man you will inherit from your father, but not from God. Not thus are born those who go to heaven: *ex Deo nati sunt.*[26] They must be born again of God. It has been announced. *Qui renatus non fuerit ex aqua et Spiritu Sancto non intrabit in regnum Dei.* The true son of God is he who is born of water and the Holy Spirit. "Unless a man be born again of water and the Holy Spirit, he cannot enter into the kingdom of God."[27] St. Paul says: He who has not the spirit of God, is not of God. He is not the child of God and he will not be saved.

Hard words indeed! Wait, for I have not yet finished! There are many of you here to whom this doctrine seems as new as if you were not Christians; and having heard these words of Jesus Christ for the first time, you go home wondering if what you have been told is true— *Omnis caro feonum, et omnis gloria carnis quasi flos agri: exsiccatum est feonum et cecidit flos, quia Spiritus Domini sufflavit in eo.* Isaiah spoke in a loud voice saying: "All flesh is grass, and all the glory thereof as the flower of the field. The grass is withered and the flower is fallen, because the spirit of the Lord hath blown upon it."[28] He was told to cry these words in a loud voice that you might all hear. So if any of the young men or young women here think a great deal of themselves, consider themselves fine gentlemen or grand ladies, or imagine that they are in the bloom of youth, tell them that they are mistaken; that they are all as grass, and that even the gentlest breeze would wither them. When the gentle breath of the Lord blows upon them they will fall to the earth.

Do any of you understand this: *All flesh is grass?* What does flesh mean? *Verbum caro factum est.* Augustine says in his book 12 *De civitate Dei,* that "by flesh we mean a man in his entirety, taking the part for the whole."[29] By this I do not merely mean man's exterior, but the whole man. Isaiah *cried* it, for there may be some who although they do not delight in clothes, in finery, in the pleasures of the flesh, are perhaps more misled than those who walk openly towards perdition. The prophet says that the "whole of man," including his sensitivity and his intellectual powers, "is grass and all the glory thereof as the flower of the field."—What is the honor and glory of the flesh? Take the case of a philosopher who from his writings seems to be a creature come down from heaven: you will find in him clear powers of reasoning; you will find that he is an enemy of vice and a lover of virtue. This is honor and glory; this is the highest aim that man can attain, better than riches, better than honors. But I tell you that this glory is as a flower of the field.

Oh, how many of you there are—brethren, now is the moment for dismay—who are confident that you are pleasing to God! But when you are called to judgment you will not be able to remain standing, because when the breath of the Lord blows upon you, you will fall. Your narrow judgment of yourself "searching Jerusalem with lamps,"[30] those examinations of conscience when you considered not only your sins but also your good works, the alms you gave, the *Pater Nosters,* the *Ave Marias* you said, the Mass you celebrated or heard, your good intentions of doing good works: all this you thought would provide some consolation for you in the hour of death. But I tell you that "all flesh is grass." The day will come when the Spirit of the Lord will blow upon these things, and they will not be able to remain upright, because they will not have the strength. Why will they be unable to remain standing? Who will defend you from God's judgment of yourself? Do you think you will be able to defend yourself? No one can protect you from God except God Himself. The breath of God will wither the flower. Which means that if you gave alms, if you pardoned injuries, if you celebrated or heard Mass, it will all be of no benefit to you, if what you do was not inspired by God.

"I do not understand," you say. Well, let those who are priests listen and be afraid. The children of Aaron said: "Let us offer incense to God; for He is angry, so that He may be pacified." They do well. They took the thuribles and lit them with the fire of this earth, instead of the fire which God had promised to send them. They began to offer incense and not only was their offering not accepted, but God killed them then and there, and they were carried out dead, vested in their linen tunics, because they had not used the fire of God.[31] God had commanded them not to offer sacrifice with ordinary fire, but with fire which He would send them; they did not obey His instructions properly and they received the punishment for their crime. Woe to the priest who goes to the altar if he has not within his heart the fire of God! Woe to the priest who says Mass or officiates at funerals, with the fire of this world within him, the fire of envy or vanity, and not the fire of the love of God! Woe to him, for he will be asked: "Tell me, the good you did, what heart inspired it? Was it thy heart or Mine?" Whatever has not been inspired by the fire of the love of God, will not be received by Him. I am not here to discuss whether deeds neither good nor bad in themselves or deeds morally good but not rooted in charity are meritorious: it is enough that whatever has been accomplished without the presence of the Holy Spirit will not be accepted. Neither the performing of miracles nor the shedding of one's blood will be of any value, if the Holy Spirit is not present. Oh Virgin Mary, how many people will be disappointed on that day!

"If any man have not the Spirit of Christ, he is none of His." How do you feel when you hear this? Let us pause. God dwells in this place. From here your hearts are judged. This judgment is a prefiguration of what God will do on the day of the Last Judgment. God says: "If any man have not the Spirit of Christ, he is none of His."

But wait: did you not tell us what was said by St. Paul?—What God incarnate preached is not more true than what St. Paul wrote.—Is there then no difference between Christ and Paul?—The tongue, the throat, and the voice are Paul's but the words are Christ's. St. Augustine says in one of his sermons: "A sower went out to sow wheat, carrying his seeds in a basket so inferior in quality that at times it was filled with mud. But the wheat was good: so it is clear that the quality of the wheat is not determined by the quality of the basket in which it is carried."[32] Saint Paul, Isaiah, Jeremiah, do you know who they are? Baskets which carry the seed and the word of God. You must not despise the seed because the basket is inferior. The Council of Trent, which I am told is in confusion at the moment on account of all our sins, approved all the books of the Bible except the third and fourth books of Ezra. What St. Paul wrote in his epistles is as true as Christ's discourses in the gospel, for the words of both are inspired by the same Spirit.

How do you feel about the Day of Judgment? Some rejoice at the thought of it, others groan. How do you feel about these words? "If any man have not the Spirit of Christ, he is none of His." There will be some who on hearing they have the Spirit of Christ will bless God, because they trust that through His mercy they have the Spirit of Christ: others will have a heart attack, especially those who imagine that the Spirit mentioned is the devil, like those pagans who could not bear to hear it said that God exists. The Jews indeed acknowledge one God, but when they heard that this God had a Son, equal to the Father, then the devil entered into them and they said: "This Man has blasphemed, for he has called himself the Son of God."[33] Christians acknowledge one God, whose Son is equal to the Father: but if you mention the Spirit to some of them, they will have a heart attack. How are we to speak if not as God and the Scriptures speak? People so inimical to the Spirit, that they cannot bear to hear Him mentioned! What is the root of this? Because their hearts are perverted. What do you do when you hear something you find unpleasant, and you are told: "God has said it"? What did Achab say? This Micaiah "doth not prophesy good to me, but evil."[34]—I am a mouthpiece. Is it my fault? God wills that this should be said to you.

The sermon which does not upset and impress you profoundly is not the word of God, nor is it listened to as the word of God. *Domine, Deus meus es tu, exaltabo te et confitebor nomini tuo: quoniam fecisti mirabilia, cogitationes antiquas fideles.* "Amen. Lord, thou art my God, I will exalt thee!" To praise the word of God is to praise God Himself. "I will . . . give glory to thy name for thou hast done wonderful things, thy designs of old, which thou hast thought of since eternity, thou hast accomplished." What can this possibly mean? *Quia posuisti civitatem in tumiltum, urbem fortem in ruinam, domum alienorum, ut non sit civitas, et in sempiternum non aedificabitur super hoc laudabit te populus fortis; civitas gentium robustarum tenebit te.*[35]—I will exalt Thee, my God, for Thou has put the city in a tumult. Thou hast stirred up that city of wickedness which existed undisturbed in man's hearts. I praise Thee because the heart which Thou hast agitated, had accepted sin calmly and without protest. Neither rhubarb nor cassia disturb the bowels like the word of God. None can hope to be consoled by God, without first being frightened and distressed. If you wish to be consoled you must suffer pain and fear. If the preacher's words do not put you in a tumult, they are not inspired by God.

I am sad indeed, because I am told that "no fornicator or unclean or covetous person hath inheritance in the kingdom of Christ and of God."[36] "Come," you may say "it cannot be quite as bad as they say; for God is mercy." You try to find excuses so that although you do not kill the word of God by denying it, you injure and weaken it, like those workers in the vineyard who killed and wounded the servants of the Lord. He denies and kills the word of the Lord who says: "I do not wish to hear this. It is no concern of mine." He weakens it who says "When I get old I will be virtuous." They try to find excuses so as not to be upset by the sermon. They are, however, upset by it, but in a short time they will return to their former pleasures and forget what they have heard.

Why do they behave thus? "The light is come into the world." Blessed be God for it! Who, then, is the light? Jesus Christ, the word of God, is the light by which you must judge your soul: "and men loved the darkness rather than the light."[37] May God preserve you from the man whom you wish to waken out of an unhealthy sleep, who, when you put a lighted taper before his eyes, puts it out, so that he can go to sleep again.—Why do you hate the word of God?—Because it spoils that dream you are enjoying. You have been told: if you do not forgive everyone his brother from your hearts God will not forgive you.[38] What will he suffer, who is at enmity with his neighbor? We are told: "Unless you become as little children, you shall not enter into the kingdom of heaven."[39] What will the proud man suffer? What will he suffer who has in his possession another man's goods, when he hears the words: "If any man has stolen from another, the devil holds him in his power?" What must you do? Put out the light and sleep to your heart's content! Remember that to sleep thus will destroy you; will send you with all speed along the road to hell. It hurts you to give up sin, and say the word of God is true. You would prefer "darkness (which is sin) rather than the light."

What are you to do? If the word of God distresses you, do not put it out of your mind! When you have a poultice on an ulcer, you do not take it off, for it will cure you. If God speaks words which hurt you, place them on the sore.—But what He said made me unhappy?—Be unhappy, make yourself weep, do something.—But I was mortified by His words. Brethren, these words will cure you, and you will see what great consolation you will receive from them later on. You are even upset to hear the words "He who has not the Spirit of Christ is none of His." Think over them. Dwell on them. How do you feel about them? You are indeed in dismay.

He who lives by his own spirit, does not belong to Christ. You are not to live according to your own intellect, your own will, or your own judgment; you are to live in the Spirit of Christ. You must have received the Spirit of Christ. What does the Spirit of Christ mean? The heart of Christ. He who does not possess the heart of Christ, does not belong to Christ. To His Spouse Christ says: *pone me ut signaculum super cor tuum, ut signaculum super brachium tuum; quia fortis est dilectio sicut mors.*[40]—Put me as a seal upon thy heart, as a seal upon thy arm. I myself must be the seal. Soften your hearts like wax and sign them with my seal, and *put me as a seal upon your arm.*

What does this mean? It means that, as St. Paul says, the predestined must "be made conformable to the image of his Son, Jesus Christ."[41] How are they to be like Him? *Ambulate in dilectione, sicut et Christus dilexit nos.*[42]—Give me, O Lord, Thy heart, and I will love what Thou lovest and abhor what Thou abhorrest.

He who does not possess the heart of Christ, does not belong to Christ.—Strong words!—Not at all. Oh brethren, you have heard many sermons and you do not yet know the things that concern you.—We are deeply distressed, Father.—That is what I want, brethren, and what God wants.—What must I do? How can I be at peace? How do I know if I am pleasing to God? How do I know if I have the Spirit of Christ?—That is good. How will you know? I am now addressing friars, priests, and those who lead secluded and retired lives. If you want to have scientific proof that you are in the state of grace, to be as sure of it as you are of the articles of faith, it is true that you do not know if you are in the state of grace. But we are talking of a knowledge that comes through conjecture and symptoms, that reveals itself through a profound peace and tranquility of soul. He is unfortunate—I do not called him damned, but in danger of damnation—who does not feel this consolation, this confidence, who cannot say "I will be saved." There is nothing sadder than to know of someone who has not this consolation. That merchants and dealers, that married persons, and those who are engaged in earthly occupations should not have this consolation given by the Holy Spirit would not be surprising; but he who has entered into an agreement with God; he who talks to God, and to whom God speaks (for when we read of God He talks to us, and when we pray, we are speaking to Him[43]), he who is close to God and is nevertheless disconsolate, his sorrow and wretchedness are indeed great! To go to the altar and receive sweetness and taste none! To light a great fire within our breast, and feel no heat. That indeed would cause us great disappointment and great suffering. If you feel thus you are indeed unhappy. If you ask a married woman: Tell me, woman, what kind of man is your husband; is he gentle or harsh? And if she says to you: I do not know at all, you would say: Well, who else would know? If you ask a priest who has dealings with God, what God is like and he says to you that he does not know, you would wonder who else you should ask.

Ipse Spiritus testimonium reddit spiritui nostro quod sumas filii Dei.[44] The Spirit himself with His consolation, His ardor, "giveth testimony" and says "that we are the sons of God." Do you see now how it is that one knows by conjecture? Keep your distress until the right moment. "When the Paraclete cometh," says Christ, "he shall give testimony of me."[45] Are you distressed? So were the apostles, because Jesus Christ was going away from them. You, too, are distressed because Jesus Christ has left you on account of that sin you committed. "Why are you sorrowful?" "Because I have offended God; because I have been ungrateful towards Him, and have struck Him." "Are you sad?" Good! Wait a little, for in eight days' time One will come to comfort you.

You go to a confessor or preacher: "Father, comfort me!" Do you want to receive consolation where you are, so that you will not have the trouble of going out to look for one that will console you? Well, the Holy Spirit will come to you—He who loves the widow, the orphan, the distressed, and the afflicted. Do you want to receive Him? I promise you that He will come into the inmost recesses of your soul; tonight I shall sleep without a care in the world, although you may think that I am not telling the truth.

"Father, how can He console me, when I am suffering so much?" That is how you will see that He is God. If the Holy Spirit were not greater than Christ as Man, He could not have consoled the apostles' grief at the time of Christ's departure; He could not have filled the gap left by His absence. Notice the sadness of the apostles at the absence of Christ, the Man! Well, they received still greater consolation from the Holy Spirit. There is no anguish no matter how great which the Holy Spirit cannot relieve.

Brethren, this Comforter will come. But you must make some preparation to receive Him. What must a man do in order to possess the Spirit of God? This is the business we must devote ourselves to this week. Free yourselves from earthly cares so that you may receive in your hearts the Spirit of Christ. I should say "of Jesus Christ" because the Spirit of God proceeds from Him as God and dwells in Him as Man.

"Father, will I be given the Holy Spirit?" It is not fitting that I should tell you that. Let Him tell you who will give you the Holy Spirit. Once, during the Feast of Tabernacles, Christ was in Jerusalem—it was in the month of September—and He was preaching in the Temple. While He was preaching, He was filled with fervor and He began to get excited and vehement and to raise His voice in His burning desire to save souls. Who would not wish to have heard Thy voice, Oh my King! Thou art rightly called the voice and the mouthpiece of the Father, for Thou couldst not have spoken more loudly than at the moment when Thou were conceived; who would not wish to have heard Thy voice and have seen the burning ardor in Thy face!

Lord, although it is a long time since Thou didst preach we can still hear Thee distinctly. Thou didst speak for those of Thy time and for all those who came after Thee. *Si quis sitit, veniat ad me et bibat.*[46] He was in the Temple during the Feast; and the following day, which was the most solemn of all, He spoke, not as He usually spoke, but in a loud voice. "If any man thirst, let him come to me and drink. He that believeth in me, out of his belly shall flow rivers of living water." May He who spoke them then speak them again now to your soul.

Brethren, why are you dying of hunger and of thirst? *Quare appenditis argentum et non in panibus, et laborem vestrum non in saturitate?*[47] Why do your hearts resemble hell—where no desire is gratified? Are you in distress? Come to Him and He will console you. If you are thirsty He will give you to drink. *Perdix fovit quae non peperit:*[48] —"the partridge hath hatched eggs which she did not lay." The partridge lays her eggs. Another partridge comes to the nest and sits on these eggs. When the mother returns, she is not allowed to approach the nest. Finally the little partridges are hatched out. But the next time the mother comes back, the birds, true to the instinct given them by God, leave their foster mother and go off with their real mother. Oh wicked animal! Robber! Demon! Why do you hatch the eggs of God? Lust, ill-will, why must you usurp a soul created and redeemed by Jesus Christ?

If you are negligent you will become the children of sin, and let yourselves be stolen away from your real parent. You are children of God. Heaven is for you. Well then, Christians, redeemed by Jesus Christ, listen to the voice of your true parent! Listen to the voice of Jesus Christ, who, on the Cross, with great suffering gave you life. Hear Him calling you! "If any man is thirsty, let him come to me and drink." Come to Me and I will give you peace and I will satisfy you. If man was reasonable he would say: "This is my Redeemer; This is He who gave His blood for me; I will go to Him." He will give you His Spirit to drink, You will be so content, so satisfied that "out of your belly shall flow rivers of living water." Not only will you gain living water and peace for yourself, but you will have enough to give to others. He is anxious to give you His Spirit: He has destroyed Himself in order to give you what you have need of. Have no doubt of this. There is no doubt on His side.

"Well, what must I do this week to prepare myself to receive Him?" "Do what the apostles did!" "What do you mean?" You know that the Holy Spirit is no friend of the flesh. The doctors of the Church say that one of the chief causes of Jesus Christ's departure was the apostles' great love for His sacred humanity. "Let Him go away," says the Holy Spirit, and "then I will come." Thou art jealous, Oh Holy Spirit! And of Whom? Of the pure flesh which was conceived by Yourself?

Let those who are living in concubinage, let the sensual see the error of their ways, for the Holy Spirit will come to neither. The bird that left Noah's ark took a green twig from an olive tree and, unwilling to place its feet on dead bodies, it returned unsullied to the ark. The raven eats dead flesh. The dove has a horror of it. The dove is a symbol of the Spirit, and the Holy Spirit has no concern with flesh that is corrupted. Free your hearts from carnal desires! Fast this week those who have the strength for it! He who wants meat, let him eat what is killed for some time and made thin with fasting. And I ask you, as a favor, to sweep your houses carefully with your Confession, for you are expecting a Guest, and He must not find your house unswept.

"Is there anything else?" Food for the hungry! You have people in your household and you must give your servants enough to eat. Remember the poor in your district and give them food this Pentecost. Since God gives Himself to you, you should give at least a little charity in return. Remember that the first fruit of the Holy Spirit is charity; feed the hungry! Give a gown to the naked; give a shirt to him who needs it! Release prisoners from prison!

"I cannot afford to give charity." Then forgive injuries! Pray to God for those who persecute you, comfort those in sorrow, suffer with the downfallen, make the troubles of others your own, for this is true charity.

"Is there anything more?" Nothing more except that when your house is swept and made inviting, you must ask Him to come. Do not be like some ill-mannered persons who say "Lord come to my house," when they have made no preparations for a visitor and the table is not even laid. First get your house ready and then ask Him to come. "Lord, by the blood which Thou didst shed for us, send us the Holy Spirit as You promised!" Say the *Pater Noster* and the *Ave Maria* seven times in honor of the seven gifts of the Holy Spirit. I am asking very little of you. Make an effort to do more! But at least these prayers every day from now till Pentecost, praying not merely with your lips but with your hearts. Beg Him to come, and He will give you

His grace in this world and salvation in the next, *ad quam nos perducat.* Amen.

Notes

1. Cf. Phil 2:21.
2. Rom 15:3; cf. Ps 68:10.
3. Cf. Heb 9:24; Jn 14:16.
4. Jn 15:26.
5. Jn 16:2–4.
6. Lam 3:33.
7. St. Jerome, *Comm. in Joanem* C. 3. ML. 25. 1137. Cf. In Is., 1. 1; ML. 24, 40; 1, 2; Ib. 74.
8. Lam 3:32.
9. Cf. Jn 16:6.
10. Jn 14:28.
11. Jn 16:7.
12. Cf. Jn 15:26.
13. Preface of the Ascension.
14. Cf. Rom 8:9.
15. 1 Cor 3:23.
16. Jn 3:36.
17. Eccl 5:7.
18. Ps 90:4.
19. Jn 15:6.
20. Jn 3:13.
21. Is 33:14.
22. Cf. Is 29:13.

23. Jn 1:12–13.
24. Cf. Jn 3:6.
25. Jn 3:13.
26. Jn 1:13.
27. Jn 3:5.
28. Is 40:6–7.
29. St. Augustine, *De Civitate Dei.* 1, 14, c. 2, 1; c. 4, 2: ML 41, 404, 408.
30. Zep 1:12.
31. Lev 10:1–5.
32. St. Augustine, Serm. 125, 8; ML XXXVIII, 695.
33. Mt 26:65.
34. Cf. 1 Kings 22:8.
35. Is. 25:1–3.
36. Cf. Eph 5:5.
37. Jn 3:19.
38. Mt 18:35; 6:12.
39. Mt 18:3.
40. Song 8:6.
41. Rom 8:29; Eph. 5:1.
42. Eph 5:2.
43. St. Ambrose, *De offic. ministr.* 1. 1, C. 20, 88: ML 16, 50, St. Jerome, Ep. 22, 25; ML 22, 411.
44. Rom 8:16.
45. Jn 15:26.
46. Jn 7:38.
47. Is 55:2.
48. Jer 17:11.

Sermon III

Pentecost Sunday

Ad eum veniemus, et mansionem apud eum faciemus.
We will come to him and will make our abode with him
(John 14:23).

■ ■ ■

It is a serious matter to preach of God, and equally serious to listen to that preaching, for he who listens must make as much effort to understand, as the preacher does to expound. The things of heaven are so lofty and so profound, so far above human understanding, that to be able to speak of them the speaker himself must have come down from heaven. It was not for nothing that Jesus Christ ordered His holy apostles not to preach His Gospel to the world until they had received the Holy Spirit.

Isaiah was a proud man. He said that he was going to prophesy the things of God; he did not realize his own unworthiness. God came and said to him: "I shall reveal thee to thyself, so that thou mayst know thyself." God gave him some knowledge of himself; showed him what he was like, and Isaiah became so conscious of his inadequacy and his wretchedness that he no longer had the courage to speak, nor the strength to prophesy and said: *Vae mihi, quia vir pollutus labiis sum.*[1] "Woe is me! How can I speak since I am a man of unclean lips?" I am not worthy to talk of the things of God. When God saw him in this state, He sent a seraphim who took tongs from the altar and put them in the fire to draw out a piece of burning coal. With it he touched the lips of Isaiah and immediately they were cleansed.

I do not know, brethren, in what state your ears are. I do not know whether they are clean or unclean. As to my lips, I myself will testify that they are unclean and declare that they are unworthy to speak of the things of God, unless the Lord sends fire from heaven to cleanse them. Let us beseech Him to do so.

Ad eum veniemus, et mansionem apud eum faciemus. "We will come to him and will make our abode with him": We shall dwell in Him. These words were spoken by Jesus Christ to His holy apostles, but they are addressed not only to them, but to the whole world.

Our Redeemer said, "If anyone love me, he will keep my word."[2] If anyone love Me! He who does not love You, Lord, is indeed unfortunate! "If anyone love me, he will keep my word." If you have a friend who values your friendship and you say to him: "Are you my friend? I want you to do this for me." If your friend thinks that by not doing what you ask, he will lose your friendship, he will certainly carry out your wishes. Our Redeemer exhorted His holy apostles to do many things and told them that if they did not obey Him, they would lose His friendship. So true is this, that he who does not obey Christ's commands will be lost for ever. And in case the disciples should not respect His words as much as those which were said by

God, He said to them: "And so that you may not think that
these words are Mine and that what I say comes from Me,
*sermonem quem audistis non est meus, sed ejus qui misit me,
Patris.*[3] The words which I have spoken to you and which
you have heard, are not Mine, but of the Father who sent
Me. Listen to them with great reverence and respect and
obey them, because you know by whom they are spoken."

If anyone love me he will keep my commandments. Our
love of Christ will indeed be well repaid. Blessed be the
Lord! Are we to love Him without hope of reward? What
will you give us in return for our love? Christ our Redeemer
said: "We will come to him and make our abode with him."
He will be our dwelling place. Who, then, are those who
are to come? The Father, the Son, and the Holy Spirit—
because wherever the Father and the Son are, the Holy
Spirit is with Them. The Three Persons of the Blessed
Trinity. As if They were of no importance! And we will not
go away—said Our Redeemer.—"We will make our abode
with him." We will dwell there. Blessed be Thou, for ever,
and blessed be the mouth that spoke such words and gave
such consolation! Did I not tell you that we were expecting
three guests? "We will come to him and make our abode
with him." It is amazing, brethren, to see the care the Holy
Trinity takes of man; the love with which the Blessed Trinity pursues man.

You may well ask: "What is man, oh Lord, that Thou art
mindful of him, that Thou art ready to die of love for him?"[4]
If we saw a man, an insignificant creature like ourselves,
pursue the Blessed Trinity with devotion and love in the
way that the Three Persons go in pursuit of us, we should

indeed be astonished. "What dost Thou see in man, that appeals to Thee so much? Why dost Thou want to continue to love man? Is it because he is learned? Because he is good? Because he is noble?" "He is none of those things." "For what reason art Thou full of love for man? Why, Lord, dost Thou wish to dwell in men?" I will tell you: because formerly God dwelt in man and when He left him, man was lost. He wishes, then, to rescue man in whom He once dwelt.

God created the first man by taking the slime of the earth, making a body out of it, and then infused into it a soul, *spiravit in eum spiraculum vitae.*[5] God breathed the breath of life into that body. In the Hebrew version the words *in nares ejus* occur, which mean that the breath of God passed through Adam's nostrils breathing a soul into him. The word *breath* is used; God's breath gave that lifeless body a soul; because without the soul the body is lifeless. God first created the soul of Adam. As St. Paul says: *Factus est primus homo in animam viventem.*[6]

In the beginning God created heaven and earth, the stars, the sea, the sands, the fishes, the plants, and all the animals. He created the whole world; on one day He made this part of it, and on another, that part; thus did God carry out His plan for creation. When it was all finished, God said: *Faciamus hominem ad imaginem et similitudinem nostram.*[7] "Let us make man . . ." God is like a kind father who has got ready a house, filled it with furniture and handsome ornaments, fully equipped it, and says: "All I am waiting for now is for my son to come and live in his house." In the same way God created the entire universe as a gift to man and for his use. God said: "It is not good that all this should be enjoyed by no one. "Let us make man in our image and likeness."

For what purpose, do you think, did God create man? So that he might love God, and loving Him possess Him, and possessing Him, enjoy Him, and enjoying Him, become blessed. Men were created that they might enter into a state of bliss, and thus attain the end for which they were made. They must, however, observe God's rules. But men were impatient. They wanted to rush in through walls, over fences, through windows, instead of going in by the front door. They strayed, they sinned, and were plunged into misfortune. God dwelt in them when they were in a state of grace; but after they sinned, they no longer wished God to dwell with them. This shows you what happens to man when God is not with him.

Let us make man in our image and likeness. The soul resembles God in two ways. First in being immortal, because the soul is not mortal. As God will never cease to exist, neither will the soul. As God is immortal, so the soul is immortal. Secondly, man is like God in that he has reasoning powers, and that he has a spirit. As God is spirit, and the soul of man is spirit, man's soul enables him to know God. In this he is unlike the animals who have no knowledge of Him.

Man must know God. St. John says: "This is eternal life"—*ut cognoscant te Deum verum*—"that they may know thee, the only true God."[8] Our first parents knew Him. As they were in a state of grace, they had the understanding to be able to know God and they had no will to love anything save God. They carried out the divine command: "Thy will be done."[9] In them the flesh was so subjugated to the will, that it desired only what the will desired. The flesh was like a humble handmaiden who conforms to her master's wishes. It was never rebellious, never insubordinate.

Man, in sinning, in breaking God's law, lost the grace he had possessed; and what had once been a shining light within him turned to corruption. His intellect became dulled, he lost the knowledge he had of God and his will became perverse—that will which God had given him so that he might love only God, and love everything in God. Man no longer finds it easy to love God because He is God. He loves Him for self-interest. If he loves his neighbor, it is not for God's sake, but merely from natural inclination. If formerly his flesh was disciplined and mortified, today it is rebellious and insubordinate. And when God left man, the consequences were so disastrous that it is sad to reflect on them; when His brightness was removed, man was left in total darkness. Ask men of intellect, those who are considered scholars, how much they can understand without God, whether they know anything without God. They may know other things, but they cannot have real wisdom without God. Again: *Et si quis fuerit consummatus inter filios hominum, et ab illo abfuerit Sapientia Dei in nihilo computabitur.*[10] If one be perfect in wisdom among the children of men, if there be one who is considered extremely wise, yet if His wisdom be not with him, if he does not possess God's wisdom, he shall be nothing regarded. The blind whom Christ made to see were a symbol of such as these.

So it is that all that is good in man became depraved, his understanding dulled, his will weak, his flesh rebellious,

rebellious in the extreme. No horse was ever as refractory as the flesh. Is it not true? Let each one of you put your hand on your heart and you will know that it is so. It is not necessary to turn to books to prove this. The role of the flesh is none other than to rebel against reason. Has is not happened to you on some occasion that you had the intention of doing some good deed, and were prevented by the flesh? Time and time again it has happened. If you want to fast, the flesh wants to eat; if your reason wishes to obey God, the flesh refuses to obey God. If man wants to pray, the flesh will prevent him doing so, and will lead him in the opposite direction. If the spirit is prepared to serve God, the flesh is in rebellion and will call out: "Do not do it!" Our Savior Himself said it with His own lips: *Spiritus quidem promptus est, caro autem infirma.*[11] "The spirit indeed is willing," is ready to suffer, *but the flesh is* weak and rebellious. It refuses to run the course. Sin is the cause of everything being lost.

You see now who we are: if we look at ourselves in this mirror, we shall see what we are, though not what we could be. Oh brethren, what would we be like if God should withdraw His sustaining hand from us, even for a moment? We should be worse than the demons; we should commit abominations. If God permitted you to know what we could become, what repulsive, evil creatures you would see! I once knew someone who constantly implored God to tell him what he was like. God opened his eyes and he paid a penalty for this favor. He found he was so ugly, so odious, so loathsome, so unclean, that he cried in a loud voice "Lord, in Thy mercy, take away this mirror from me!

I cannot bear to see my face any more."[12] Brethren, we are become wretched and unclean. Our souls have become evil and though they have taken on the appearance of the Holy Spirit we are in reality full of wickedness and cunning. When on the Thursday of the Last Supper Judas came with a number of people intending to deceive Jesus Christ and take Him away, he was carrying lights, but because he had come to take away Jesus Christ for an evil purpose the lights did not enlighten him; his spirit remained in darkness.

How often it has happened that holy religious, happy in their monasteries in the service of God, have been suddenly struck by the thought that if they went into the desert, they would lead a more secluded life and would be quite alone. They would then be better able to dedicate themselves to God; they would progress further in their interior life than they could in the monastery, where, they are now convinced, they do nothing but have their meals, go to the choir, and spend their time unprofitably. And this thought worries them to such an extent (for they think it is a holy thought, though in reality it is evil) that they leave their monasteries to go into the wilderness in order to be able to serve God better.

A married man visits a monastery and seeing the monks there together, thinks the place so wonderful he becomes discontented with his lot, with his wife, his children and his home and with having to work—even though he may be working to support his family. He considers existence under these circumstances to be a hell on earth. In his opinion one cannot serve God anywhere but in a monastery, and he would like to undo his marriage and go and live in one. Finally he gets his way. But that is very wrong, because he has made that change only because he is lazy and does not want to work. God has called you to a certain state of life and in it you must gain salvation. Be conscientious about doing your duty, and He will give you the grace of salvation. The devil will never let you be contented if you are leading a holy life, but will make you dissatisfied in order that you may lose the peace of mind you should feel in the state to which God has called you. He will make you hope and long for what cannot be, for the impossible. Do not be credulous! Observe how easily you are deceived by revelations and inspirations! Do not let yourself be carried away by them: for every soul must be tried and these inspirations are thieves and false witnesses and more harmful to you than darkness.

There are thieves who deck themselves out in silken garments and no one who knows them would ever imagine that men with such an air of respectability could be so evil —until they are caught red-handed. Then everybody, amazed that these men are thieves, says: "Who would have thought it?" They robbed your soul and you did not know it. They took away your entire fortune and you did not miss it.

"All others, as many as have come, are thieves and robbers."[13] Jeremiah said "*Sic fures in nocte rapuissent.*" On earth, thieves when they come to steal, take a number of belongings but leave you something, either what they cannot manage to carry away, or what they overlook; but the thieves of the spirit, who come sometimes by day, sometimes by night, sometimes in disguise, rob you of everything you own, of your entire fortune, of all your possessions. Your body remains healthy, but your heart and your soul have suffered grievous injury. They searched your whole house, looked into all the corners, into the inmost recesses; nothing of value remains, they have taken everything, but they have left you full of evil of every kind. Your enemies have despoiled you, wounded you, they have attacked you as a wolf attacks sheep; you are now poor indeed. If anything remains it is your faith, but since it is no longer inspired by charity, it is decapitated and is no longer alive.

Who will put this right? Who will find a remedy for so many evils? One cannot have life without Jesus Christ. Without Him, all is death, all is deception. Who can give life to these souls that are dead?

"How shall I know, Father, that my soul is dead?"

By the kind of life your soul leads. When your soul is alive it loves and knows God and devotes itself entirely to His service. The death of the soul occurs in three ways: through neglect, through error, through the passions. In the soul that does not love God, the will, the reason, and the memory are dead. When the soul is dead, it cannot perform a good action.

Jesus Christ said: "I am come that they may have life and may have it more abundantly."[14] Jesus Christ came to give us life. May He be blessed for ever, who with His death bought life for us! He who is great and powerful came and breathed life into the little child.[15] How terrible to see Jesus Christ on a Cross, like a criminal, dishonored, tortured, insulted. Your soul is in the same state as He was on the Cross. He was believed to be evil, your soul is evil as well as sick; He was disfigured by suffering, your soul is disfigured and stained with sin; He was surrounded by executioners and thieves, your soul is surrounded by sins and demons.

Blessed be Thou, Oh Lord, and glorified be Thy name, who wished to help me at such cost to Yourself, who died, as man does, and in so doing gave me life! The sins committed by my hands were paid for by the hands of Jesus Christ. My feet led me along the ways of sin, Thine were nailed to the Cross. My heart sinned and offended Thee, Thine was torn and pierced for my sake. Finally all the Sins committed against God by my hands and feet and my heart were expiated on the Cross—His hand and feet were nailed, His heart pierced for my sake. With His blessed body He made amends for all the sins which I committed, all the offense I gave to God.

God created the first man, and breathed into his face the breath and the spirit of life, and he lived. *Et factus est primus Adam in animam viventem, novissimus Adam in Spiritum vivficantem.*[16] The second Adam, Jesus Christ, was created, and not only had He a spirit like the first Adam, but He filled many others with His spirit. Christ has a *quickening spirit:* His spirit gives life and will revive those who desire life. Let us go to Christ; let us seek out Christ, for He has the breath of life. No matter how evil, how lost, how disturbed you may be, if you go to Him, if you seek Him out, He will help you, will rescue you, will direct and cure you. "All others, as many as have come, are thieves and robbers."[17] *I am come that* those who come to

Me, those who seek Me out, those who call Me, *may have life,* may receive life and may rise again.

"Father, how does Jesus Christ give life?" He Himself said: "Amen, amen, I say to you . . . I am the door, he that entereth not by the door . . . the same is a robber."—"I am the door." Since Jesus Christ is the door, then no one can enter in to the presence of the Father, except through Jesus Christ. *Ego sum ostium, si quis per me introierit, salvabitur: et ingredietur, et egredietur et pascua inveniet.* "I am the door. By me, if any man shall enter in, he shall be saved, and he shall go in and go out, and shall find pastures."[18]

"Since Jesus Christ is the door, where will this door lead to?" "To the Holy Spirit." *I am the door.* He who enters through Me will come into the presence of the Holy Spirit. *Lex enim spiritus vitae in Christo Jesu.*[19] For the law of the spirit of life is in Christ Jesus. God planted that law in Adam's heart; it remained living for it contained the spirit; in the same way Jesus Christ placed within you His quickening spirit; it will bring you life. Thus it is fitting that the great Elisha should place himself over the little dead child, should bow upon him and lie on him and that he should want to breathe upon him. Ho who does not receive *the breath of Christ,* no matter how rich or powerful he may be, no matter how much he may possess of this world's goods, is poor, weak" and wretched, for he has not Christ. Vine and branches are nourished with the same sap; Head and body are sustained by the same holiness: the spirit of Christ and the spirit of those who are incorporated in Him, is all one. He is the vine, and His members are the branches.[20] *I am the door:* he who wishes to receive the Holy Spirit let him enter through Me!

"How shall we enter? Where is this door?" Do you not yet know the door? What a door it is, and how well painted! How well cut the stones are! How well chiselled! The keystone is the best cut of all. Jesus Christ and all His servants were chiselled by the troubles and persecutions of this world and therefore, His servants deserved to dwell with Christ.

"If He is the door, how shall we enter by it?" He who desires the Holy Spirit, let him love and obey and desire Jesus Christ forever! *Ipse Pater amat vos, quia vos me amastis.*[21] Is it of little importance that the Father should love you? There are no better chains with which to hold the Holy Spirit than by loving Jesus Christ. "Because you have loved me," says Jesus Christ, "the Father himself loveth you," because you loved Me very much. He who loves Jesus Christ and desires Jesus Christ will in return receive the Holy Spirit. The bargain God makes with us is to our advantage. And because the apostles loved Jesus Christ so much, the breath of God breathed into them on Pentecost Sunday and they were given the Holy Spirit. The breath of God on this occasion produced an even more sublime effect than when God breathed into the first man after he had been created. The apostles had been wanting in courage and determination, when God breathed into them from heaven on this day of Pentecost. And as He had created Adam from the slime of the earth, in the same way He gave new life to these apostles who were so downcast, so sorrowful, so upset, and so timid. Think about Jesus Christ!

Obey Him, love Him from the depths of your heart, so that the Holy Spirit may come to you. As He Himself said: "I am the way, the truth and the life."[22]

Through Christ we come to the Holy Spirit. The sanctity which does not pass through Jesus Christ is not real sanctity. He who scoffs at penances, he who despises the outward devotions and works of piety does not possess the Holy Spirit. What is the cause of this wrong attitude, of this mistaken outlook? It comes from thinking that there is a path of sanctity other than that of Jesus Christ. Be careful you do not fall into error! Choose the path that is holy and good and safe! If you do not go along it, all your efforts will be in vain. He is the *way*.

What effect did the coming of the Holy Spirit have on the church? What did the Holy Spirit accomplish in the hearts of those believers to whom He came? He gave them life, gave them gifts of infinite value, strengthened them, and brought them nearer perfection.

The blessed apostles were in favor with God, but they were weak; they did not dare to confess the word of Jesus Christ publicly, they were afraid; but once they had received the breath of the Holy Spirit, they were full of grace, they were strong, and without fear of any kind. They began to preach to men the mysteries of our redemption, which were accomplished by the death and holy resurrection of Jesus Christ, true God and true Man. It was impressed on them that they must always keep God in their hearts and reverence Him as the source of all good and all mercy.

Tell me, you who are in the married state, would you be envious of one who was so strong that he could take a ton weight of lead and throw it as far as the sky; who could hurl an iron bar even higher? You are distressed and sad, but you can gain reward in heaven if you bear with these griefs and hardships. Have patience in the difficulties arising from your marriage, and turn them to merit by offering them to heaven; have the strength to throw these heavy weights of lead higher than the sky. Any little trouble that may occur in your home, any inconvenience, any unpleasantness you may meet with, the bad temper you have to put up with from wife or husband, or employer, or those around you, in the difficulty you may have in supporting yourself and your family, say: "For love of You, Lord, I take pleasure in undergoing this trial!" Raise your eyes and your heart to God, commend yourself to Him, offer Him your difficulties, and I tell you truly that you will receive in exchange great reward. Offer Him your sleep, the food you eat, what you drink, let all you do and suffer be for God. Offer it all to Him, raise it up to Him! If you do this your burden will become light; the lead, the earth, will reach heaven. Do this and it is possible you will gain more merit in a single year than another in ten. That is, if you do as I say and if you are able to persevere to the end as you ought; if the thought of God and the respect for His holy presence enters into everything you do.

"The Holy Spirit," says Christ, "whom the Father will send you, will animate you and He is called the *Paraclete*, the Comforter, the Exhorter."[23] Comforter because although He reproves us at times, He does not go away without consoling the soul that He has admonished. This Comforter reproaches and reproves souls. It is as if He said: "What are you interested in? What are you doing? Why have you become neglectful of your duties? Take warning, that is bad! You must put first things first, you must avoid that company, you must seek out those others, you must consort with these people. Mind, for life is passing. Do what good you can, give what charity you can! Put into practice all that you have been taught! Do not let your life slip by merely in good intentions and pious thoughts! Put these ideals into action! Be careful! Life is going by and you do not know whether God may call you while you are still young. Take care that you are not in a fool's paradise," and a great deal more of the same. And if after this exhortation, this reprimand, your soul is overwhelmed, distressed and frightened, the voice you heard was not that of the Holy Spirit. He reprimands only that He may console us; He reprimands only that we may amend our ways and be happy to receive warnings. If after that reprimand, after your remorse, confusion, tears, and shame at sinning against the Lord, if after all that you are happy and trust that the Lord will not abandon you, that He will help you to be better and reform your ways, then the words you heard were those of the Spirit, who has entered into your heart; He has reprimanded you, He wants to console you. This is His way: to give peace after the whirlwind, to give love after fear. He who animates, exhorts, and consoles you, who teaches you how to behave in all situations, will teach you to steer and guide your bark. He will ensure your safe arrival in harbor in spite of contrary winds, for His advice and His teaching are sufficient to guide you.

What was the origin of the practice in the early church of the Christians owning neither goods, possessions, money, nor livestock? The Christians sold what they had and brought the money and laid it down at the feet of the apostles.[24] "Take this rubbish!" The great love they felt in their hearts and souls for Jesus Christ and His holy poverty made them despise everything material. Who rewarded them for their love? Who? The Holy Spirit who had come to their hearts with an abundance of gifts. Who altered such a one's nature? Who gave him so much patience? He who was once so ill-natured that no one could stand him is now a St. Jerome, with the disposition of an angel; bears meekly and in silence with everything and is tolerant of everything. It is the Holy Spirit who brings about these changes in men's hearts. In addition, He fortifies and consoles the soul where He dwells and presents it with innumerable gifts and mercies. These graces descend on us from above; there is no power on earth that can accomplish as much. No one on earth can transform hearts. No matter how inclined to evil your flesh may be, the power of the Holy Spirit for good is stronger. No matter how healthy you are, He can make you ill; no matter how flourishing you are, He can wither you; no matter how daring, he can tame you; no matter how high your position, he can pull you down. He kills within you, removes from you, all that displeases God. He fosters and increases and revives all that is agreeable to God. He fills you with zeal that you may try how you can please God; fills you with such love of your neighbors, that you feel as distressed at their difficulties and hardships as if they were your own, if not more distressed. He makes you as fleet-footed as deer so that you may run along the way of the Lord.

Who could possibly describe the marvels, the wonders, the changes of heart in the members of the early Church, which were wrought by the Holy Spirit, the Paraclete and Exhorter? We could produce many witnesses of the powers of the Holy Spirit from those days: but since we have others near at hand let us avail ourselves of them. There are many who despise the world, have no use for clothes, ornaments, pleasures, holidays, worldly pomps and amusements, have no interest in entertainments, games, jousts or tournaments, who do not wish to be seen or to see, who refuse to go anywhere even if the necessity is great (if they can at all avoid doing so) so as not to have to walk the streets and come across something which would trouble their souls, even if only for a moment. These servants of Jesus Christ give up pleasure and seek out hardships; they are free people and they make themselves into slaves. Is it necessary to search in books to prove this?

The Holy Spirit is the cause of their attitude. It is His teaching that makes them fly from the things of this world so that they may see Jesus Christ; they would rather weep and groan where they are, than rejoice in the world. This cannot be accomplished by flesh and blood alone. It is not given to flesh and blood to have such strength. Ask some lady to follow this example. She could not do it. The flesh of itself is too weak! The persuasion and grace of the Holy Spirit are needed; and so Christ sends the Holy Spirit. "Who performs these miracles?" If you see someone making this sacrifice, you are not interested so much in what he does as in the spirit in which he does it, because it is quite certain that he would give up more if he possessed more. He does not regret what he is renouncing, he regrets only that he has not more to renounce for the love of Jesus Christ. If he had a thousand worlds he would give them up to come to the feet of Christ. He would rather please God and serve Him than be lord over the whole earth.

"But why does he do this? Why does he choose this state of life? Why does he want to lead a life of seclusion?" This can only be answered by an eye-witness. So great is the zeal of the servant of God who wishes to please God, who wishes to keep his soul unspotted, that he does not trust what is trustworthy; he is even doubtful of what is lawful. It is not wrong to be married and to own your house; but because he cannot be certain that that which is good today will not be an occasion of sin through carelessness later on, he will take this surer path. How does he know he might not lose his soul amidst the upsets of life as a husband, a father, and a householder? It is as if someone said to him: "Get into this river; here near the bank it is quite shallow, and you cannot drown." "I do not want to," he replies, "because if I once put my feet into the water, I might perhaps want to go further and further out, until I come to the deep part. Then, unable to return, I should drown. I prefer not to go in at all, in case I should be powerless to come out when I wanted."

"Why did he decide to embrace this state of life?" He was shown the blood of Jesus Christ; he was shown the sufferings of Christ; was told how much Christ did for him, how much He loves him, how greatly Christ should be loved and served, and he became convinced that this was the only path for him. "Who made him do that?" "Who ordered him to do it?" God, not his own body. Flesh and blood have not strength enough for such sanctity. "Who told him to do it?" I do not know. He knows.

In the old law, God ordered the first fruits to be offered to Him. *Afferentur virgines post eam.*[25] The purity of Our Lady the Virgin pleased God so much that in the verse I have quoted Jesus Christ provided that virgins should be offered in imitation of Our Lady. Many maidens grew up who offered themselves to this celestial King, Jesus Christ; they willingly gave up all that the world has to offer, and chose Him. They were happier to possess Him than to be the wives of kings and princes of this earth. "The first fruits," says St. Cyprian, "are virgins, those in heaven who are most complete; they are complete in body and in soul; they are a symbol here of what we ought to be and what we should be like in heaven. We must enter heaven chaste and incorruptible, whole in soul and body. The virgins living here on earth are thus and *they do not live in the flesh according to the flesh.*"[26] They are the best of God's dwelling-houses among men. He delights to be in these pure hearts, free from stain and corruption. St. Jerome says "that the man who preserves his virginity and purity of body, while living in the body is higher than the angels; because the angel acts and behaves according to his nature; man with the help of grace which is above his nature. Those who are virgins have this merit. They can be called angels, because, through the gift of grace, they have the nature of angels in their corruptible bodies."[27]

This high state should not be chosen for lack of an alternative; it must be chosen only for the love of Jesus Christ, and with the sole desire of pleasing and serving Him. She is holy, who chooses it for this reason and who, in the midst of vanities, despises the world and scorns all it has to offer. He, or she, is the servant of God who turns his back on the world in youth when he could best enjoy it, at the time when he has most disposition and inclination for pleasure. These are the first fruits, the grain that is burnt. "Who has treated you thus?" "*The sun hath altered my color;*[28] love of the sun has done this to me. I am grain that is burnt brown. Within I am beautiful, outwardly I am burnt and darkened with the love of Jesus Christ." Beautiful women should not pride themselves on their good looks, if their beauty is merely external and the wickedness of hell is within them. Spouses of Christ, do not be distressed if you have lost your beauty for the love of Christ, for He will give you beauty of another kind. All that you give up for Christ's sake will be returned to you in even greater abundance. Be glad at this and if you are ever troubled by the thought of how much you have renounced, say to yourself: "Lord, if I have given up something for your sake, it is of little value. You deserve a great deal more and I must give you more."

St. Paul said to the Hebrews: *Si enim sanguis hircorum et taurorum, et cinis vitulae aspersus inquinatos sanctificat ad emundationem carnis, quanto magis sanguis Christi, qui per Spiritum Sanctum semetipsum obtulit immaculatum Deo, emundabit,* etc.[29] "For if the blood of goats and of oxen and the ashes of an heifer, being sprinkled, sanctify such as are defiled, to the cleansing of the flesh, how much more shall the blood of Christ, who by the Holy Spirit, offered himself unspotted to God, cleanse our consience from dead works, to serve the living God?" What power has this holy blood? Does it not cleanse our stains, wash away our sins? Who would not say: "Who, Lord, caused You to suffer so much? Who inspired Your heart to accept such suffering?" The blood of Christ *which was shed by the Holy Spirit:* It was the Holy Spirit that moved and incited Christ to shed His blood so readily for us. It was the Holy Spirit who said to Him: "If Thou diest not, no one will enter into heaven: die, or no one will be saved."

Do not be frightened because the Holy Spirit has brought you today to be placed on a cross; because when Christ renounced all pleasure, when He was obedient, poor, and rejected, the Holy Spirit performed another and a greater deed. He who made Jesus Christ lay Himself on a Cross, made your heart choose to follow Christ, made you renounce and forget all other pleasures. Do not regret what you have done; do not be discouraged at anything that may happen to you; because I tell you that the greater your sacrifice, the greater the temptations the devil will put in your way. The convent will seem to you a hell upon earth, the choir a market-place, your cells a prison, Mass a torment. You will imagine you are getting too little to eat and that you are being badly treated. You will say to yourself: "I had a great deal when I was in the world, and gave it up. I could quite well save my soul, even if I still owned and enjoyed it all." Innumerable temptations will come to overthrow you; be on your guard! May God make you understand how little you have given up and how much you will receive!

Do not let yourself be deceived by the world, maiden! For what anguish, what despondency, what sufferings, what worries are hidden by that facade of pleasure. He who thinks about it will say that he is indeed happy to be free of the world. May God make you understand that you will not lose by what you have done but will benefit from it; that far from having chosen the wrong course, you have chosen the only right one!

Did not David ask to escape from these dangers? *Averte oculos meos, ne videant,* etc. "Turn away my eyes, Lord, that they may not behold vanity."[30] He meant that the eyes which should look at God should not look at worthless things. What we love dearly we take care of. Avert your eyes from vanity, for they hope to see God! You cannot see God with eyes that look on vanity. Put your feet in the stocks of the cloister, and your neck under the yoke of obedience; make yourselves captives for Christ's sake! Place yourself in irons for love of Him, and remain constant and you will feel less confined than if you had the whole world to move about in. What good is space if your soul is confined? Suffer willingly and faithfully the hardships which come to you through His will! He will repay them and will let you know that you will receive benefits as a reward. Woe to him who has not these dispositions!

Let none of us think it wrong that you should leave money, father, brothers, home, and pleasure for God's sake; on the contrary to do that is to gain the highest honor of all. I should prefer to receive, if I could choose, the hardships and insults which St. Paul suffered for Jesus Christ rather than the favors, and revelations he received—for the latter are of less value. Fortunate maiden, who have given up the world so that you may gain heaven, you will receive more than you have renounced. How shall I express it? You come in here to serve; you will be served by Him. Put your feet in the stocks of the cloister and spurn the chain of gold; although your feet may be suffering hardships, repelling the world, raise your eyes to the honor which is prepared for you; look at your crown, look at your reward!

It is related in the *Lives of the Fathers* that a certain monk saw a procession of saints, some of whom wore very handsome gold chains around their necks. He was told that they were the reward of those who had bent their necks under the yoke of obedience. Obey, maiden, abase yourself, serve, sweep, work as hard as you can! The harder you work here below, the more magnificent and the larger will be your chain of gold in heaven. Deprive yourself here on earth, that you may have wealth there! If you are lonely on earth, you will later be the companion of those who enjoy God; if you close your eyes here, you will see God in the next life; if you work here below, you will rest in glory for ever.

Notes

1. Is 6:5.
2. Jn 14:23.
3. Jn 7:16.
4. Ps 8:5; Heb 2:6.
5. Gn 2:7.
6. 1 Cor 15:45.

7. Gn 1:26.

8. Jn 17:3.

9. Mt 6:10; Lk 22:42.

10. Wis 9:6.

11. Mt 26:41.

12. Cf. M. de Roa S.J., *Life and Marvellous Virtues of Doña Sancha Carrillo.* (Seville 1615). 1. 1. C. 9, 17 R–5.

13. Jn 10:8.

14. Jn 10:10.

15. 2 Kings 4:34.

16. 1 Cor 15:45.

17. Jn 10:8.

18. Jn 10:9.

19. Rom 8:2.

20. Jn 15:5.

21. Jn 16:27.

22. Jn 14:6.

23. Jn 15:26.

24. Acts 4:34.

25. Ps 44:15.

26. St. Cyprian, *de habitu virginum*, 3. 22–23; ML 4, 455.

27. St. Jerome, Comm. in Is. 1, 16, c. 59; ML 24. 597.

28. Song 1:5.

29. Heb 9:13–14

30. Ps 118:37.

Sermon IV

Pentecost Sunday

Paracletus autem Spiritus Sanctus . . . But the Paraclete,
the Holy Spirit . . . (John 14:26)

■ ■ ■

"He that is of the earth, of the earth he speaketh. He that cometh from above is above all," said St. John the Baptist to his disciples.[1] They were slightly envious because more people were following Jesus Christ than their Master; and to appease them He said these words: "No one can receive anything from heaven, unless it be given him from heaven. *He that is of the earth, of the earth he is, and of the earth he speaketh.*"

He that is of the earth is commanded to ascend to heaven. But how can he? How can he rise to heaven? What is a man to do who is commanded to speak of heaven? He cannot possibly obey. It is something he could never do of himself, as impossible as it would be for the earth to rise to heaven. *Qui de terra est, de terra loquitur.* If we were told to speak of ordinary things, of the things of this world, we should acquit ourselves well; but how could we talk of such a lofty theme as the Holy Spirit, or of the things of heaven, we who are less than dust? What would enable us to speak of holy matters?—The grace of the Holy Spirit. It was not

72

given in vain to the apostles to help them to preach. *Audivimus eos loquentes variis linguis magnalia Dei.*[2]

The blessed apostles were filled to overflowing with the fire of the Holy Spirit; they were filled with this celestial grace, so that it might be understood ever after that no one should speak or preach of the Holy Spirit unless he be filled, and filled to overflowing, with this heavenly gift, with this holy fire. When the apostles spoke and told of the marvels and wonders that witnessed to God's greatness and published them abroad, they were glowing with fervor and filled with grace sent them by Our Lord. The Holy Spirit came in tongues of fire so that they might understand that the tongues of those who speak of the wonders of God must speak words of fire, words of burning love. These tongues when talking of God and His greatness must not speak words that are insipid like the water, empty like wind, nor words that are of the earth.

We come to listen to the word of God, we come to sermons with no more love or reverence of God than if we were going to a play. I tell you in truth that those of us who listen to sermons run a great risk; we shall be in great danger if we do not listen as we ought, with our hearts ablaze, and our souls on fire. We are come together here to hear about the Holy Spirit and to speak of Him. For such important business we need to have grace, we need the Holy Spirit to infuse Himself into our hearts, to soften them and set them alight with the gift of His divine fire. St. Paul says "that the Spirit himself asketh for us with unspeakable groanings."[3] The prayer which is not inspired by the Holy Spirit is of little value; the prayer which does not conform to His wishes, which He has not inspired and directed, will bear little fruit, and be of little use.

Christ said to his apostles: "But because I am going now sorrow hath filled your hearts. But the Paraclete, the Holy Spirit, whom the Father will send you in My name will console you. He will teach you all things and bring them to your mind, whatsoever I have said to you."[4] He will open your ears so that you may hear, and enlighten you so that you may understand: He will teach you to pray and to do all things which you should do, so that you may choose the right way in all things. We have great need indeed, of this Paraclete, of this Doctor, this Counsellor, this Teacher.

What must we do so that we may have Him? Let us go to the most holy Virgin. She is deeply loved by the Holy Spirit and He by her. In her womb the incomprehensible happened; He that is great and mighty humbled Himself; He that was from eternity made Himself mortal; He that was rich became poor: and all this was accomplished through the power, the operation, the direction, and the wisdom of the Holy Spirit. The angel Gabriel said to the Virgin: *Spiritus Sanctus superveniet in te.* "The Holy Spirit, Lady, shall come upon thee and the power of the Most High shall overshadow thee."[5] The Holy Spirit is within the womb of the Virgin; He knows her purity of heart; He knows the temple of her body where He accomplished so many and such great mysteries. The Virgin never thought or spoke anything which could in the least degree offend the Holy Spirit; she was always pleasing to Him and always carried out His holy will; through the petitions of this holy Virgin, through her supplications, entreaties and prayers, the Eternal Word came to her womb.

Let us beseech her who is so loved by the Holy Spirit to obtain for us the grace to speak of this important guest.

Si Spiritum Sanctum accepistis credentes?[6] "Have you received the Holy Spirit since ye believed?" St. Paul enquired of some Christians. Have you received the Holy Spirit? Do you possess Him within you? Blessed be the soul who has received Him! Blessed be he who by believing has received this guest! He gives Himself to man in return for man's faith in Him. Not only had these not received the Holy Spirit but they said: "We have not so much as heard whether there be a Holy Spirit." The Holy Spirit had not been given to them. Perhaps there may even be some here who have not heard whether there be a Holy Spirit. Oh, if only you would answer truthfully! Have you received Him? Do you love Him? Have you served Him? Do you desire Him? Do you long for Him to be infused into your hearts? You do not even know whether there be a Holy Spirit. Merely to deserve Him is of no use. It is not enough to ask Him to come, to wish to receive Him, unless your actions merit His coming to you. *Factis autem negant.* Your deeds must be in harmony with your conversations and your desires, if this great guest is to come and dwell in your soul.

Many have preached of the Holy Spirit; many prophets spoke of Him very many centuries ago. Scripture says that the Spirit of God moved over the waters: *Et Spiritus Domini ferebatur super aquas.*[7] All the prophets understood and revealed great secrets and mysteries concerning the Holy Spirit. Among them was Jesus Christ—and He more than the others testified to Him; He related such marvelous things of Him that they were all amazed to hear them.

Said Jesus Christ to his apostles: "Let not your heart be troubled; nor let it be afraid . . . because I go!"[8]

"But Lord it is quite the contrary; it is because Thou art leaving that they are troubled. What new kind of love is this? What is this new way Thou hast of treating those who love Thee? Thou art going, and they love Thee more than the light of their eyes: Thou dost want to go, and to console them for Thy departure, Thou sayest to them: *Let not your heart be troubled because I go.* It is precisely because they know that Thou art going away, that they are troubled and distressed."

No one can understand or follow this if he has not the Holy Spirit. "You have been comforted by Me; you have been happy with Me, you have been taught by My doctrine, you have been fortified in My presence. *I go, and I will ask the Father; and he shall give you another Paraclete* in my place.[9] Up to the present I have comforted you; now that I am leaving I will send you another Paraclete, someone to replace me." "Oh, powerful God! Who is this Paraclete whom Thou wilt send?" "The Spirit of Truth who will dwell within you, and teach you not wrong ideas and false doctrines, but the truth!"

May the skies and the earth bless Thee, Oh Lord! God the Father was not contented merely with sending us His only beloved Son, our Lord Jesus Christ, to die for us. He came Himself. Jesus Christ said: *Si quis diligit me, sermonem meum servabit, et Pater meus diliget eum, et ad eum veniemus, et mansionem apud eum faciemus.*[10] "If any one love me, he will keep my word. And my Father will love him, and we will come and make our abode with him."

Study and ponder over these words and carry out this order and obey it! This promise is a proof and a pledge of His love. And, brother, tell me, in what dispositions do you listen to the Word of Christ? Are you attentive? Or do you take your ease when the preacher speaks to you of Him? Are you glad when you hear His name mentioned, when He is spoken of, praised, blessed, and glorified from the pulpit? But you are more interested in some made-up story, in some recent news. You listen to that kind of talk with the greatest attention.

He who keeps my word, loves me. What does this mean? How am I to keep His word? How am I to show my love for Him? You must love Him; and to show that you truly love Him, you must reject and renounce all that prevents you from loving and serving Him worthily. "If thy right eye," if something you prize as greatly as you do your eye, or "if thy right hand, scandalize thee," if anything you consider essential should make you deviate from this holy purpose, "cut it off."[11]

"Terrifying words! Strong words, Father." You must have by you a sharp knife, and if father or mother, brothers, relations, friends, or anyone else should separate you from the love of Jesus Christ cut them down, do not spare them, walk over them; trample them under foot, and though this may appear to you cruel, it is quite the contrary; it is godliness.[12] If you sin because of money, or possessions, for the sake of relation or friend, to dishonor or to honor someone, to gain favor, or to destroy, for death or for life, cut it off!

"Harsh words. Am I not allowed to desire the wife of another? Am I not only to refrain from taking another man's goods but ordered to give my own? Am I not only to refrain from doing harm to others, but to do all the good I can? This is a harsh command. Lord, make it easier for me! Thou dost want me to work and toil at this most difficult task when even by making every effort, I can accomplish very little. Promise me some consolation, some reward!" "I will." "My Father will love him," says Jesus Christ "and as a reward for obeying Me and carrying out My commandments—thus repaying them for the hardships they have endured—the Eternal Father will turn His eyes upon him 'and we will come to him and make our abode with him.'"[13] It will not be merely a brief visit, He will make His dwelling place and mansion there.

Could anyone read these words without blessing and praising the Father, the Son, and the Holy Spirit, who are coming to dwell with him? Do you want more? Are you content? Will you continue to chase shadows, to seek money, honors, to want to go up in the world, to become important, to gain high positions? Do you want more than this? St. Bernard said: "Oh hearts so hard that even this knife cannot cut them, nor this fire burn them, nor this goodness move and curb and soften them!"[14] Since the Son, the Father, and also the Holy Spirit are ready to come to you, you cannot from now on call yourself an orphan if the world does not honor you, or make much of you, if you do not prosper and become rich here on earth.

"Lord, do You intend to give us even more?" "I will ask the Father; and he shall give you another Paraclete."[15]

This astonishes me more than anything else. The disciples were waiting for this Paraclete; they desired Him so greatly that though they did not know who this Paraclete was, nor what He was like, they loved Him deeply and longed to see Him. "I will ask the Father; and he shall give you another Paraclete."

"Lord, what words of wisdom come from Thy mouth? What will this Paraclete be like, who is coming to console us for Your absence, who will comfort and teach us and do all that You do?

It is not difficult to guess how happy Christ made His disciples; what joy they felt in His presence. Merely to look at Him banished their worries. No mother ever loved and cherished her children as Jesus Christ loved and cherished His apostles; no bird ever cared for its young, protected and sheltered them under its wings as Jesus Christ looked after His own. He loved them deeply, spoke with them, taught them, comforted them, advised them, removed their fears, gave them strength, gave them innumerable benefits. And they loved Him so deeply that for His sake they gave up possessions, money, the nets with which they earned their living; husbands left their wives, sons their fathers, and some women their husbands. He was so loving to them, and His conversation was so gentle, so full of affection, that they would have given a thousand worlds for one hour with Him. How confident, how happy, how joyful they felt when they were with Christ! Those who saw Jesus Christ with their own eyes and heard His holy words with their own ears may indeed be called rich and fortunate, and rightly so.

Jesus Christ said to them on the Thursday of the Last Supper: "Your hearts are troubled because I have told you that I go away."[16] Those fortunate ones were so happy to be with Jesus Christ that it seemed impossible that anything could ever console them if they were separated from Him; impossible that anyone in the world could fill the gap caused by His absence. They were dazzled, they were enraptured by His holy person and by His presence. They believed they would be inconsolable once He left them. Who would comfort these apostles in their great sorrow? Who would make up to them for their loss? Who would cure the wound which Christ's absence would cause in their hearts? It was a grievous wound caused by love, and it would take a great deal to cure it.

"When I go another Paraclete will come to comfort you." But could anyone replace Jesus Christ? He tells them that He wishes to go away, and to alleviate their grief and their sorrow promises that He will send another Paraclete. "Then you will no longer grieve because I go. Another Paraclete will come equal with Me, who will comfort and cherish you even more than I."

Only God could heal this wound, and this is a powerful argument to believe in the divinity of the Holy Spirit. Because if the Holy Spirit were less than God, He could not comfort the apostles in the sorrow they felt at Christ's absence. Jesus Christ is God: if the Paraclete who was to be sent were less than Christ, He could not be God; and therefore would be unable to console the apostles. It is clear, then, that since Christ said He would send them a Paraclete who would be able to console them, as He could, this Paraclete must be God, as Jesus Christ was God. No one but the Holy Spirit could fill the void in their hearts, for He, like Jesus Christ, is God.

Therefore you must take heart, because if you call Him, He will come to your aid in any difficulty you may have. You complain "I am being accused. People are talking about me. I have lost my money. My husband has left me. I am suffering greatly and am very ill. My friend has been disloyal. I am miserable. I am beset with temptations. There is great dryness in my heart. I do not know what is wrong with me, I am continually faced with difficulties, and am constantly in danger of death." Have patience! Do not give way to despair! Bear up! You will not be abandoned. Call this Paraclete, who will comfort and guide you; since His presence was sufficient to console the apostles' sorrow at the loss of Christ, He will also console you, for their loss and their distress was greater than any you can possibly experience. Compare your sorrow with theirs and you will see that He who could console them in their overwhelming grief can solace you as well.

Has this Paraclete come to you? Has this Guest arrived? Has this great day dawned for your house?

"Father, I do not know what is wrong with me. I used to be so pleased with life, now I am discontented; the joys and pleasures of this world make me sorrowful; games, passtimes, entertainments, indeed all earthly delights, are distasteful and abhorrent to me."

If the day has come when you feel like this about the world, you must give thanks for it and be grateful to the Lord. He who receives this Guest within him, he who receives this Paraclete despises and holds in contempt the things of the world, and all that is prized by the worldly. He is repelled, satiated, disgusted, saddened by all earthly joys.

Learn how to call this Comforter, try to please and delight Him; because he who has this Guest must never treat Him unceremoniously. Such a Guest should receive every attention. Say to Him: "Lord, I am happy with Thee: Thou alone art sufficient to satisfy me; I need no one except Thee and having Thee I have everything; if Thou art with me, all others may fail me; if Thou dost comfort me, the whole world may treat me badly; if Thou art on my side the rest may be against me."

"Where is this wisdom to be found?" Within the heart of God. Answer me this: When Christ went away, were we left orphans, did we remain alone, abandoned with none to advise us? What was our position? Did He send another in His place? Let the preacher who, through His mercy, knows the answer, tell you and may God make you understand!

How great are God's mercies! How marvelous His works! May He who can make you understand what you have lost, when you lost the Holy Spirit, also make you understand how quickly you can regain Him. It is indeed a calamity and a great privation to be unaware that one has suffered such a loss. The evil is even greater if you do not repair that loss, when it is possible to do so. God loves you; He wants to bestow favors upon you, to send you His Holy Spirit. He wants to fill you with His gifts and graces and I cannot understand why you should consent to lose such a Guest. Why did you give your consent? Why did you let such a thing happen? Why do you not lament such a loss? Why do you not call out to the Lord?

How shall I explain to this congregation the relationship the Holy Spirit wants to establish with your soul? It is not incarnation exactly; but a state where the soul is united with God in a union so close and so complete, that it resembles incarnation; although from another aspect, it is very different from incarnation. The incarnation was a union in which the divine Word united in His one person the divine and human natures. But this is not the case in our union with the Holy Spirit, for we are joined to Him in a union of grace. The former union is called the incarnation of the Word, and the other may be called *spiritualization* by the Holy Spirit.

Today the Holy Spirit preaches the same message that Jesus Christ preached, teaches the same doctrine, consoles and delights man as He did. What more could you ask for? What more could you look for? What more do you want? For you have within you a counselor, a tutor, a director. One who will guide you, advise you, encourage you, put you on the right road, who will accompany you in everything you do, and everywhere you go. Finally, if you do not lose sanctifying grace, He will go by your side so that you may neither do, say nor think anything that is not inspired or directed by Him. He will be your faithful and true friend; if you do not leave Him, He will never leave you.

As Christ during His life on earth performed marvelous cures among the sick who needed Him and asked for His help, so this Teacher and Paraclete performs spiritual cures among those souls in whom He dwells and with whom He is in union through grace. He makes the lame walk, the deaf hear, the blind see, puts the erring on the right path. He teaches the ignorant, consoles the afflicted, strengthens the weak. Christ, as man, went among men performing these holy deeds, which He could not have done if He were not God, so we say that they were the work of God and Man. And we call the wonders accomplished by the Holy Spirit in the heart where He dwells, the work of the Holy Spirit and man, though man here plays a lesser part.

If a man does not enjoy this union, has not this Guest in his house, has not this counselor, this guide, this protector, this tutor, comforter and guardian, do we not consider him unfortunate and unhappy? And since you have not got Him within you, you are as you are—distressed, sad, listless, full of bitterness, lacking in piety, miserable. Tell me, have you received Him? Have you called Him? Have you besought Him to come? Have you sighed and wept for Him? Have you fasted? What prayers have you recited? May God come to you! I do not know how you can bear to live without His great goodness. Remember, all the benefits, all the graces and mercies which Christ came to bring to man, are given to our souls by this Comforter; He preaches to you, cures you, teaches you, and gives you innumerable blessings.

Has it never happened that your soul has felt dry, lacking in fervor, discontented, full of fear, sorrowful, disillusioned, so that nothing can satisfy you; and while you are in distress, and perhaps distraught in mind, a breath of holiness comes to you, a feeling of relief revives you, strengthens, encourages you, and makes you yourself again; gives you fresh aspirations, ardent love, great and holy peace, and makes you speak words and accomplish deeds that astonish you yourself. That is the Holy Spirit.

That is the Comforter who has breathed upon you, has come to you, without warning of any kind. You will be as if touched by a loadstone; you will have renewed vigor, will act and speak differently, and have new desires. Whereas formerly nothing seemed of importance, everything worried and annoyed you, now you have a zest for living, you are content, everything exhilarates you, you learn from everything. A blade of grass, looked at attentively, will make you praise Our Lord, God, and will teach you to know the Maker and wonderful Creator of all things, and will so inspire your heart with feelings of piety and gratitude towards the all-powerful Lord, that if you could speak you would tell of the marvels and wonders performed by the Lord of Creation.

Oh happy Paraclete. Oh blessed breath of God that wafts vessels to heaven! The sea which we have to navigate is full of perils; but with Thy help and with Thee as pilot we shall arrive safely. Many boats will be destroyed! Contrary winds will blow! Dreadful dangers await us! But when this holy Paraclete breathes upon these vessels, they will arrive safely in port. Who could possibly estimate the favors He has bestowed on us, and the dangers from which He has safeguarded us? The breath of the Holy Spirit comes from heaven and returns there to the Father and the Son; it blows from thence and the Holy Spirit, breathing upon His friends, guides them and brings them to heaven, for it is His wish that they should go there.

Christ said to his apostles: "Stay you in the city."[17]

"But why, Lord? Shall we not go forth and preach? Why must we remain here? Are we unworthy?"

Before this Comforter arrives, before the breath of the Holy Spirit comes upon us, we do not exert ourselves, we are sluggish, we feel despondent, everything appears difficult, impossible. There seems to be no way for us to get to heaven. There are obstacles everywhere and we feel as if we were carrying a stone of lead. A stone did I say?—A hundredweight of lead. How can dead bones come to life? How, being dry, can they be covered with flesh and rise again? It is clear that, of themselves, they are powerless, but God, who can do all things, can cover them with flesh, and infuse into them the spirit of life, and make them rise again, and give them the power of movement and energy.

God called the prophet Ezekiel and said to him: "Son of man, dost thou think these bones shall live?" Can they have life and be covered with flesh and sinew? Ezekiel answered, "Lord what Thou askest me, Thou knowest." And God said: "Behold, dry bones, I will send spirit into you and you shall live. And I will lay sinews upon you and will cause flesh to grow over you and will cover you with skin; and I will give you spirit and you shall live. And you shall know that I am the Lord."[18]

Every man who has not the Holy Spirit is dry bone, hard and without marrow or virtue, dead bone. But after the prophet had called upon the divine breath to blow upon those dead bones, they regained life; they were transformed; what was heavy became light, and the dead became alive. You were evil, cast down, without the fire of charity, inanimate, and you showed neither kindness nor tenderness to any one; you were overcome with weakness, incapable of doing good of any kind, inert as the dead. In this state, God says to you: "Man, do not be frightened! Do you imagine that you will not be able to rise again? Take courage, because I have more power to save you, to revive you, to give you life and make you happy than all your wickedness has to overthrow you, to destroy you, to kill and dispirit you. If My power for good were not stronger than yours for evil, your sins would finally damn you and make you thoroughly wicked."

May the skies and the earth bless Thee, Almighty God! In a little time many will bear witness that their vessels were on the verge of being lost, were about to be broken in pieces, and would have foundered, when Thy breath blew upon them and rescued them and they arrived safely in port. Many who have lost all hope of life, have been revived by the Spirit, have been given life and new desires, have been cheered and strengthened by fresh hope! By whom is this accomplished? By the Holy Spirit, who breathed upon them and brought them unresisting to God.

What more does He do? Who can find words to describe all that He has accomplished? The apostles were thrown into prison, scourged, and ordered not to preach, and they went away smiling and *rejoicing* and considering themselves fortunate *because they were accounted worthy to suffer hardships and reproaches for the name of Christ our Redeemer.*[19] Remember how St. Peter, for fear of a little servant-girl, denied Jesus Christ three times, saying: "I know not the man."[20] But after the Paraclete came, after this divine breath had touched his heart, neither threats, nor prisons, nor bonds, nor scourging, nor death itself could stop him from preaching and confessing the holy name of Jesus Christ. St. Paul said when in prison: "Do not think that because I am in prison, I am unhappy; I tell you that here where I am, I receive comfort not only for myself, but sufficient to be able to send you all consolation."[21]

Jesus Christ says in his holy Gospel: "If any man thirst, let him come to me and drink."[22] "What do you mean, Lord? What water have you that will quench the thirst of those who come to you?" No waters or springs could ever refresh the thirsty as effectively as the Holy Spirit of Christ. He will take away the anxieties and the thirsts of this world and will extinguish the ardent desires and the craving for the things of the earth. That is why Christ, Our Lord said: "If any man thirst, let him come to me and drink." And if a man comes to Him and drinks of the water of the Holy Spirit and receives this Paraclete, this divine breath of the Holy Spirit, he will be filled, he will be comforted, he will be taught, he will be preserved from all error and doubt.

St. Bernard says that He will teach you everything; sometimes when alone with you—at other times through the mouth of another. He is anxious to instruct, console, help, and strengthen you. If there were many disciples who wished to be taught this doctrine, who wished to study in this school, they would all be able to learn of this gentle Spirit, source of all wisdom.

In other schools, although a man may be evil, he can leave fully instructed in his own speciality; but in this school only they will profit by the teaching of the Holy Spirit and be accepted as His disciples who are the *ablactatos a lacte, avulsos ab uberibus:* "them that are weaned from the milk, that are drawn away from the breasts of their mothers:"[23] these are taught by the Holy Spirit. He is in communication with them; He gives Himself to them. Have the courage, brethren, to wean yourselves for God's sake! Have the courage to draw yourselves away from your mothers' breasts, so that you may become disciples and students of the school of the Holy Spirit! Wean yourselves from your own will, from your own judgment! Renounce and depart from your nature, your own opinions!

My Lord and my God, if Thou art not our friend, if Thou dost not help me, if Thy powerful hand does not sustain me how can I do what Thou asketh? How could I separate myself from, wean myself from, abandon, the things of the world? But with Thy help I can. I will. Nothing will stand in my way. I will forget the world, despise everything in it and cast it from me. I would prefer, Lord, to suffer for Thee, than to be happy in the world! I would rather weep than laugh, since Jesus Christ our Redeemer promised a great reward for suffering when He said with His own lips: *Beati qui lugent, quondam ipsi consolabuntur.* "Blessed are they that mourn for they shall be comforted."[24]

It happens sometimes that infants die when they are weaned. Some people like their children above all else, others prefer treasures and riches, others honors, others position and high office, others privileges, others their wives and husbands; each one enjoys and delights in the pleasures of his choice. Make up your minds, brethren, to give up, to wean your hearts from, to remove yourselves from whatever you like best in the world! Sometimes when an infant is weaned it becomes sickly. Take courage, brethren, and if there is something which pleases you particularly, give it up for our Lord God's sake, and say: For love of Thee I wish to renounce this pleasure, this consolation, this thing that pleases me so much and that other one that particularly appeals to me; if there is anything Thou, my Lord and my God, wishest me to put out of my mind, to abandon, to surrender, to perform, I will conform to Thy will; help me, my Lord and my consolation; give me strength, give me help!

Accende lumen sensibus—infunde amorem cordibus— infirma nostri corporis—virtute firmans perpeti. Light Lord, with the rays of Thy eternal brightness, the darkness of my understanding, so that I can with confidence and a clear mind choose Thee alone for my eternal good, and may forget all other things since they are merely shadows and illusions. My Lord and my God, set my heart and my will on fire with love and desire for Thee, so that I may love Thee alone, seek only Thee, so that I may cling only to Thee. Let my eyes rest only on Thee, and may Thou never allow me to stop loving Thee! And because the weakness of the flesh prevents us from carrying out our resolutions as we ought, strengthen, Lord, with Thy strength, the weakness of my body, remove my wicked sensuality, change my evil ways, so that all that is within me may please and content Thee, may understand, love, and serve Thee!

"Father, I have heard so much good of this Paraclete, of this Guest, whom we are to receive within our souls. Tell us why He is to come, and what He will accomplish within us."

It would take a long time to answer that. Who could count the favors He gives those He visits? He brings innumerable gifts. He performs many works of mercy in the soul that surrenders itself completely to God! Christ our Redeemer performed miracles, cured the sick, made the dead to rise, and preached. Who could possibly enumerate all the favors which Jesus Christ our Lord heaped on mankind? Well, the Holy Spirit does as much for souls. He heals those sick, He makes the dead to rise and makes the dumb to speak so that they may tell of the greatness of God, Our Lord. Who wants to receive this Guest? Who wants to have this Counselor, this Paraclete?

"But, Father, will He want to come to me?" Listen: *Omnes sitientes venite ad aquas: emite absque argento; et absque ulla commutatione, vinum et lac.*[25] "All you that thirst, come to the waters, and you that have no money, make haste, buy and eat. Come ye: buy wine and milk without money and without any price." He mentions *water* first, then *wine* and *milk. Water* because it quenches the thirst and cools the body, invigorates tired limbs, and washes away all uncleanness. *Wine,* because it will make you leave behind your own mind, and adopt that of Christ. It will take away your own opinions and your own will, and substitute for them the opinions, the will, and the desires of Jesus Christ Our Lord and Redeemer. Who wishes to receive Him? You can buy Him without payment! He is like *wine,* because He gives strength and courage to suffer hardships for Christ's sake, because He cheers us, and makes us happy in the midst of adversity. He is also like *milk,* because the Holy Spirit treats the soul of him who possesses Him like a mother her infant, and directs, controls, and cherishes it, exactly as if it were a child; thus He is guardian, protector, teacher, to us His little children.

Who wants to receive Him? Who, among you, brethren, wants to receive Him? Who desires Him and is in a state of grievous sin? Who asks Him to come while His heart is elsewhere? The glorious apostle St. Paul said to the Ephesians: *In quo et credentes signati estis Spiritu promisionis, qui est pignus haereditatis.*[26] What use is there in being baptized and believing in Jesus Christ if I have not the Holy Spirit? If I have not this pledge of our inheritance, of what value is all the rest? Without the Holy Spirit neither baptism nor calling myself a Christian is worth anything. As circumcision was the outward sign of the Jew, so is baptism the outward sign of the Christian, but neither baptism nor anything else can save you if you have not the Holy Spirit. And the *sign* of salvation and the sign by which you will gain what Christ has promised us is not merely to call yourself a Christian, to be baptized. You must have the Holy Spirit. Those who are baptized and have not the Holy Spirit are children of God, but not legitimate children. They cannot therefore inherit from the Father, because illegitimate children may not inherit, though they may receive gifts. He who is baptized and does not obey God, Our Lord, as also he who has not the Holy Spirit, is not a legitimate child of God. He is illegitimate, because he has not the *sign* which makes children legitimate, and enables them to inherit the goods of their Father who is the Holy Spirit. *In quo et credentes signati estis.* When you received the outward sign of Christianity and when you received the Holy Spirit, you became one of Christ's flock, and were marked as one of His sheep, one of His fold. If we have not the Holy Spirit, we will not have an everlasting covenant, as it was promised by God to Isaiah: *Feci vabiscum pactum sempiternum misericordias David fideles.*[27]

Who desires Him? Who desires Him? Call out the good news! Who desires this Guest? Who desires this Paraclete?

All are not ready to receive this Paraclete, all are not ready to receive this Guest, especially those who have the reputation of being wise and sensible. "I should have to stand before him, like Jerome," says the youth: "I could not get about, I could not talk, or enjoy myself, I could not go to games and entertainments, nor where I wanted. I should always have to stay within bounds. I should find this excessively trying. Who could stand it?"

"Ah, Lord what is this I hear? We are to ask petitions of Thee, and not to love Thee! Thou art to give Thyself to us without payment and we are not to esteem Thee! Since Thou, Lord, knowest how important it is for us to receive Thee, and how much we shall lose if we do not receive Thee, explain this to us and make us understand."

A woman who is with child does not jump nor do heavy work, lest she endanger that which is within her; but a lively young girl who is not pregnant will skip and dance and play full of confidence because there is no danger where she is concerned. Do you want to know whether you possess the Holy Spirit or not? If you notice that you have become forgetful of duty, that you go where you want, laugh and talk, and enjoy yourselves, it is a sure sign that you have nothing of value to lose; we could perhaps prophesy that you will soon lose the Holy Spirit, since you lack the love of God. It is a sure sign that we possess something of value, if we make an effort to keep it and are afraid of losing it. And if your friends say to you: "Look at this!" and you answer: "I dare not." Or say: "Let us go there!" "I dare not." "Let us have a good time!" "I cannot." "Let us go off and do something!" "I dare not," they will ask: "What is the meaning of this? Who has influenced you? Who has taken away your liberty?" "The holy fear and reverence for this Guest whom I have within me has bound my hands and feet, and imprisoned my desires and my heart; I am so enslaved that I can neither do nor like anything that is not pleasing to Him, and that is not His will."

He who is waiting for this Guest, or who already possesses Him, puts himself in bonds, in order to be more worthy to receive Him, to give Him a better welcome or, if He should have already arrived, to keep Him in his heart and prevent Him from leaving. "Why will you not go there? Why can you not be like other people? Why are you so annoying? Have more assurance! Be of some use." If you see someone behaving in such a way as to call forth remarks of this kind, if you notice he is preoccupied, cannot answer for himself, cannot defend himself, you can be sure that man has the Holy Spirit in his heart; this Guest dwells within him; for these are the signs of the Holy Spirit. *Notite contristare Spiritum Sanctum.*[28] Be careful! "Grieve not the Holy Spirit of God" who dwells within us. He who has a great lord as his guest is careful of what he does. He dare not leave him to go off to parties and games. He would be worried about his guest. "Who will look after him?" he would say: "Who will give him his meals? Who will see that he is safe? I must go home. You will have to do without me. Don't depend on me! Forget me!" If you have not this anxiety to please your guest, this fear and reverence for the Holy Spirit, you will be completely undisciplined. You will run, enjoy yourself, play jokes on people, eat and drink, not caring whether you lose Him, going to no trouble to prepare for Him and receive Him. How tragic that would be. If you wait for Him, desire Him and long for His coming, what matter the trouble you take. No man, no matter how poor he may be, if he heard that a king was coming to stay with him, would not borrow or somehow obtain a few hangings and ornaments with which to decorate his house. "I have just heard that a king is coming to my house. What am I to do? Lend me some hangings, some draperies to make it look more attractive! Even though I am extremely poor that is no reason for my house to be bare of ornaments, dirty, and uninviting."

When you are asked to do something sinful, when you are faced with some temptation, answer: "I am waiting to be cleansed; why should I make myself unclean? I am waiting for my Lord; how could I leave my house?" *Non permanebit spiritus meus in homine, qui caro est.*[29] And St. Paul says: *Nescitis, quondam membra vestra templum sunt Spiritus Sancti?*[30] Be careful, for your eyes, your hands and your mouth, are the *temple of the Holy Spirit;* do not defile the dwelling of the great Lord! If you indulge your carnal appetites, the Holy Spirit will leave you! The Holy Spirit cannot bear to remain with a soul that is defiled; the two cannot live together. There is no middle course; you have to choose one or the other. If you choose the Holy Spirit you must rid yourself of all sin, of all blemish; and if you choose to remain in sin, the Holy Spirit will leave you. Consider then, whether it is preferable to possess the Holy Spirit, the Paraclete, in a heart free from sin, or to lose this ineffable good for pleasures that are experienced by the beasts of the field. You are not risking or losing very much when you renounce what is wrong for what is right when you give up falsehood for truth; when you give up uncertainty for certainty. Since the choice you are faced with is clear, and since so much is at stake where you are concerned, you do not need to ask advice about what you should do. You can make up your own mind.

Who desires Him? Remember He gives Himself without payment. He does not ask much of you. In veneration of the Holy Spirit who on this day came and infused Himself into the hearts of the apostles, from this time forward, reverence and honor this Guest, serve Him faithfully; even if sorrows come to you, try to work to make Him happy; even if you have to sleep on the floor, give Him your bed; and even if you have to suffer hardship, do what you can to please Him. For love and reverence of Him, I ask you to honor Him. Do not give yourself over to the devil! Do not exchange this Paraclete for anyone! You cannot live without either the Holy Spirit or the devil. What a difference between these two guests! Let us bless ourselves when we hear the devil mentioned! Will we refuse to bless ourselves when through mortal sin we have him within us, since we are at enmity with God?

Let us look attentively at the apostles and observe with what faith they awaited Him. These blessed apostles were expecting the Paraclete: like them you should perform works of mercy and do good to everyone you can at this time. They were locked in, together with the blessed Virgin Mary; call her, win her over, as that other widow importuned and won over Elisha.[31]

I have been reflecting that since the Holy Spirit came to those who crucified Christ, He will come now to those who call on Him with piety. It is indeed amazing to see the gentleness and love with which He taught the apostles to preach and pray. St. Peter says: "Brethren, you have sinned, know your sins and do penance for them, for the Lord will pardon you and send you a gift. Get ready your hearts to receive it."[32] May God reveal your hearts to you, your inward disposition so that you may recognize your sins! May you hear of that voice which is louder than an organ—may you be aware of that perfume which is stronger than civet—may your conscience reveal your sins to you and make you weep for them! With your whole heart call on Our Lord, Jesus Christ, and if you do this the Holy Spirit will come to you. Do you want the Holy Spirit to come to you? Call Him in the name of Jesus Christ. The Holy Spirit has so much love for Jesus Christ that if you call Him in His name, He will come.

"He is pure: how could He come to me who am unclean?" That is the question. Why has the Holy Spirit so much love for Jesus Christ? Because Jesus Christ placed Himself willingly on the Cross, in obedience to the Eternal Father and the Holy Spirit; which is why the Holy Spirit will come to you in Christ's name, and will not be repelled by your wretchedness. He will not fail to come; He will not show contempt for you. Who would ever think of mixing gold with mire, purity with refuse, the valuable with the worthless, the lofty with the despicable, such great goodness with such frailty and such insignificance? You see it is quite true that man is not a suitable dwelling for the Holy Spirit, just as the Cross was not the place for our Redeemer, Jesus Christ; but through this union with the Cross, has come about the union of the Holy Spirit with man. The Holy Spirit advised and inspired Jesus Christ to put Himself in that mean and repellent place—the Cross; and because He did so, the Holy Spirit will come to that other mean, repellent place—the heart of man. Beseech Him to do so, entreat Him! Call Him in the name of Jesus Christ, our Lord, because He will most certainly come and give Himself to you, and present you with all His gifts. He will enlighten your understanding, He will make you burn with love for Him, and will give you grace and glory.

Notes

1. Jn 3:31.
2. Acts 2:11.
3. Rom 8:26.
4. Jn 16:6, 13; 14:26.
5. Lk 1:35.
6. Acts 29:2.
7. Gn 1:2.
8. Jn 14:1, 27.
9. Jn 14:16.
10. Jn 14:23.

11. Mt 5:29; 18:9.

12. Cf. St. Jerome, Ep. 14, ad Heliodorum, 2 (ML 22, 348) *Licet parvulus ex collo pendeat nepos, licet sparso crine et scissis vestibus, ubera, quibus te nutrierat, mater ostendat, licet in limine peter iaceat; per calcatium perge patrem, siccis oculis ad vexillum crucis evola. Solum pietatis genus est, m hac re esse crudelem.*

13. John 14:23.

14. St. Bernard In fess. Pentec., serm. 2, 8 (ML 183, 330). *O duri, et indurati et obdurati filii Adam, quos non emollit tanta benignitas, tanta flamma, tam ingens ardor amoris, tam vehemens amator, qui pro vilibus sarcinulis tam pretiosas merces expenditis.*

15. Jn 14:16.

16. Jn 14:27–28.

17. Lk 24:49.

18. Ez 37:3–6.

19. Acts 5:41.

20. Mt 26:72; Mk 14:71; Lk 22:57.

21. Phil 1:3ff.

22. Jn 7:37.

23. Is 28:9.

24. Mt 5:5.

25. Is 55:1.

26. Cf. Eph 1:13.

27. Is 55:3.

28. Ep 4:30.

29. Gn 6:3.

30. 1 Cor 6:19.

31. 2 Kings 4:1ff.

32. Acts 2:38.

Sermon V

Pentecost Monday

Non enim misit Deus Filium suum, ut judicet mundum
(John 3:17).

■ ■ ■

There are two powerful incentives to the completion of any task: to understand the aim to be attained and to be confident of success. When we despair of achieving some aim, we make no effort to find a way of carrying it out. We do not even begin to try.

I have asked myself on more than one occasion what is the reason why so few seek the Holy Spirit; why so many never trouble to ask themselves "have I the Holy Spirit?" They eat, enjoy themselves, attend to their business; they all completely lose their heads over every pretty woman they see, while the Holy Spirit, with all His beauty, has few lovers who would lose their sleep on His account.

How much sleep has your anxiety to have the Holy Spirit cost you? It is incredible how few there are who love and desire this Spirit, though His rewards are so much greater than those of the world. Many would willingly lose their honor, their sleep, would perjure themselves for a silver coin, while they care nothing for the riches of the Holy Spirit. Why do we not go in pursuit of these riches?

God said through the mouth of Moses: "Do not say: this commandment is far above us. Which of us can observe it? Which of us can go up to heaven for it, or which of us will go down to hell to bring unto us? But the word is very nigh to thee, in thy mouth and in thy heart."[1] St Paul said: "Say not: Who shall ascend into heaven? That is, to bring Christ down; Or: Who shall descend into the deep," *id est, Christum a mortuis deducere,* "to bring up Christ again from the dead?" *Sed prope est verbum in corde tuo et in ore tuo. Hoc est verbum fidei quod pracdicamus.*[2] Do not be perturbed, he says, and ask "who shall ascend into heaven" to bring us salvation from there, *id est,* Jesus Christ? "Who shall descend into the deep" to bring Him up from there? Who would not wish to be near Him, and able to enjoy Him and receive salvation from Him? "Do not say this," says St. Paul, "for He is nigh, even in thy mouth, in thy heart." If you have faith, you will be saved.

But to come to our point. There will certainly be some of you here most anxious to see the Holy Spirit. You probably say: how much I should enjoy having Him, when the apostles were so desirous of seeing Him, because of what Jesus had told them about Him, that they were beside themselves with anxiety! What you must not say is: "How could I ever see such goodness? Am I not longing for something I can never possess! I love a being so far above me that I despair of possessing Him. He is truthful, I am a liar. He is pure, I am unpure. He is great, I am insignificant. How could He love me?" Do not give way to anxiety! Do not despair! If only you long for Him and desire Him, He will do the rest.

Daniel saw a *stream of fire* flow downwards.[3] How could such a thing happen! Is it not the nature of fire to rise? Did not the Apostle say that it was fitting that Christ, having suffered for us, should rise to heaven and seat Himself at the right hand of His Father, *ut appareat vultui Dei?*[4] Why should this be, Lord? Jesus Christ had to do this, so that He might appear in the presence of the Father for us, show Him His wounds, offer Him His sufferings and say to Him: "Eternal Father, since Thou lovest me, love these my children, for whom I have suffered." The Holy Spirit comes through the merits of Jesus Christ: He comes from His face and countenance. Jesus Christ being the face of God, we use the word face because it represents and is a figure of the divinity of God, an image of God: *Qui cum sit imago Patris et figura substantialis ejus.*[5] What does the word "come" mean if not to run downwards? Did the Holy Spirit not come from heaven to earth? Does this not mean to descend? This stream of fire which is the Holy Spirit runs down, descends to the vileness of men.

Today the Holy Spirit comes to hearts and sets them on fire and inflames them. Have no doubts about that: Christ gained infinite merit for that very purpose, and it is through Christ's merits that the Holy Spirit comes. Just as when God came as man and entered the womb of a woman, the Blessed Virgin, she had prayed to Him and asked Him to come, and in answer to her supplication He came to her, entering her womb, and sanctified her and blessed her, He will also come to us in answer to our prayers.

May God grant you have a holy Feast of Pentecost and receive great graces from the Holy Spirit. It is fitting that

we should preach today on some words written by the
Holy Spirit with the pen of the Evangelist St. John. They
were sung during the gospel of the Mass. They are gentle
words; all the more so since they were spoken by Christ.
Here they are: "For God sent not his son into the world to
judge and condemn the world; but that the world may be
saved by him."[6] He must love the world, since He sent such
a person to it. He must esteem this jewel, since He pays
such a high price for it. Those of you who know Latin, do
not fail, on any account, to read that chapter; it seems to
me the gentlest that the Gospels contain.

See how the Lord talks with Nicodemus! He was a
good man, an educated man. Among many other things
which you will read there, He said to him: "I say to thee
unless a man be born again, he cannot see the kingdom
of God." Nicodemus asked Christ: "How can a man be
born when he is old? Can he enter a second time into his
mother's womb? Art thou a master and a doctor in Israel
and knowest not these things?"[7] You may be very well educated, but as regards how to attain salvation, you are quite
ignorant. You do not know what 'to be born again' means?
Then you cannot see the kingdom of God. To see it, is to
enter it. St. Augustine says: he who is unborn cannot see
the things of the world; nor can you see the things of God,
unless you be born again.[8]

And thou knowest not these things? Have you not read in
the Law, in the Book of Numbers, that when the children
of Israel murmured against Moses God sent serpents to
kill them, and when Moses himself interceded with God
for them, asking Him to take away that plague, he was told

by God to set up a serpent?[9] This is the truth of that image, the reality of that sign. "I had to be placed high on a Cross so that all those who looked at Me and raised their eyes to Me with faith, should have life. And if you are amazed that I should do so much for your salvation, it is not through your merits." Do you know the reason? *Sic Deus dilexit mundum.*[10] *God so loved the world.* What emotion do you feel when you hear these words: *God so loved the world as to give his only begotten son,* who knew that what He did for the world would cost Him His life? How God loves me! My soul is so dear to Him, so precious to Him, that He sent His only son to His death, so that I might not be lost!

Lord, who could be proud of ancestry, possessions, station in life or beauty? You should be ashamed to have honor and glory, you who are so loved and wanted by God. Did He send His only Son so that we might be lost? Could there be a higher honor than to follow Him who loves you so much? Could you have a stronger motive for so doing? The reason why so many do not serve God is that they do not understand how much God loves them. They do not know what He did for them; that He gave His son for them; that He wept so that they might have happiness and contentment. Are you not glad to hear the words: God loved you very much. It was Himself who said it. God sent not his son to condemn the world, or to *judge it;* if He came for this, who would escape? Who would not be condemned? No. He came *that the world may be saved by him.*

"It seems, from this, that the world was lost before He came." "Yes, and before He comes to the soul, it is lost." "How was the world lost?" "Let us learn the answer to that, because it may perhaps show us the road to salvation." *Homo, cum in honore esset, non intellexit, co mparatus est jumentis insipientibus, et similis factus est illis.*[11] God created the world, adorned it with trees, plants, and animals. He created a man and a woman. He made them the lords of creation. He put them in charge, in a place of privilege. The greatest honor He gave them was to create them in His own image and likeness and to make them subject to Him.

But man when he was in honor did not understand. He was unable to keep free from sin. More strength is required to remain virtuous in success and prosperity than in adversity. You need more grace to prevent you from falling when you are in a position of importance than when you are brought low by misfortune. Man did not value what he possessed. He wanted to rise higher, and because what he desired was beyond his reach, he lost the privileges he already had and destroyed himself. Not only did he lose God, abandoning Him for his own interests, but he lost his humanity. He who is in sin is less than a man. He is lost, *made like to senseless beasts,* since he renounced grace and was disobedient to God. In sinning you seek what your appetite and your flesh desire. Would you not agree that a man is he whose life is guided by reason and natural intelligence? What would you call a gentleman who is dressed in fine silks and brocades, but who at heart is a beast? What would you think of a man who is, apparently, in command of others, but who is himself influenced and ruled by a beast? There is no greater dishonor than to be in sin; through sin, man becomes a beast. *Non intellexit.* He did not understand what the trials of a beast amounted to, the burdens, the hardships, the fatigue, etc. Through sin, these troubles came to the world. Through sin, greed, honors, rights of succession came into existence.

Do you remember the story of the madman who built a great city to so fortify his kingdom that God would not be able to put him out of it? Nebuchadnezzar was his name. "Who," he asked, "could take my power and dominion from me?" Well then, wait! He hears a voice from heaven: "Thou wilt be thrown out of thy kingdom and thy house and for seven years thou wilt be like a beast among beasts, grazing as they do, and seven years will pass over thee, till thou knowest that the power of the Most High is in heaven and not in cities, nor brick nor stone."[12] *Datur ei cor ferae,* it seemed to him he was a beast. He left his palace and went into the fields with the beasts and stayed there seven years. What is the meaning of this? Seven periods of time will pass over you until you know that the power of the Most High is in heaven, not in cities, nor in stones. Since you took away honor from God, not only your kingdom but even your heart will be taken from you, and you who have been made a man will find you are less than a man. So it is that because you abandoned God, not only were grace and virtue taken from you, but a beast's heart was given you.

What? Does this not happen among us every day? Because for a time you were devout, given to prayer and contemplation, impervious to temptation, you became conceited, and trusted in your own strength. The kingdom was taken from you, you no longer knew how to be devout or to pray, nor who God was; you became like a beast so that you might learn that what had been given to you was a great favor, and one to which you had no right. Now you have forgotten the word of God, and all that is good. Know yourselves. The lion knows the man who feeds him, as does any animal. You do not even know that? May the heart of a beast be given you; may you receive no mercy. This is what Job said in the name of sinners: "The things which before my soul would not touch, now, through anguish are my meats."[13] Because Adam and Eve sinned, all their descendants are born in sin.

God says: "Leave these madmen be, for I will let seven years pass over them; I will give them to understand how little they are worth without me." St. Augustine says: "Let men try out their strength thoroughly and let them recognize their weakness, and let them call on God's help, and seek aid."[14] But human nature intervenes and makes them do the opposite. Knowing what they should do, they did not do it. Knowing what was right, they did what was wrong; knowing what was evil they did not avoid it. The law was written in their hearts. They did not keep it, but it taught them that they were doing wrong. They said: "If we had a law, if there were someone in command, then we would obey." God gave them six hundred and sixty commandments so that they should not complain there was no law; and not only were they sinful, but they were even worse than before, because they had been given the law. *Lux subintravit ut abundaret delictum.*[15] Not because the law was bad, but because of the wickedness and frailty of human nature. Rid yourselves of this wrong opinion of yourselves. Know yourselves to be weak and evil.

Oh, how often do we say: "I am engaged on some business at present and I am not going to confess the fact, or even acknowledge in my conscience that I am doing wrong. Tomorrow when my business is finished, I will confess this sin." And later on, not only do you leave unconfessed those sins which you are now committing, but you add others to them.

This foolishness and presumption, this confidence in our own strength will destroy us. Indeed man lost himself through his desire for greatness and sank below the level of the beasts. And in the seventh year, after men had been treated like beasts as a punishment for their sins, God sent the Savior of the lost, not to judge and chastise them— *non enim misit Deus Filium suum,* etc., but that the world may be saved, may be put right by Him.[16]

We have come to the heart of the matter. How can man be saved? He had sunk below the level of a beast and was now less than a beast. How can he be rescued? Let this beast's heart be taken from him and let him be given another heart in its stead. Whose heart? Not a man's heart, but God's heart. Through sin, man lost his human heart. Let his beast's heart be taken away. Shall he be given a man's heart? *Aufer a nobis cor lapideum.*[17] Today is the day when man is recreated, renewed, when the beast's heart shall be taken away from the world, and the heart of God given in its place. In former times, baptism was administered only on the Feasts of the Resurrection and of the Holy Spirit, so that the people might understand that baptism is a resurrection of the spirit. Today's feast has the same effect, because it is the day when men receive new hearts from

God. Today the children of men become the adopted children of God. This is the day.

Listen to me carefully! How did Jesus Christ save mankind? Have you observed how He fought for us when He was on earth, arguing with the Father, pleading with Him for us, offering himself for us? He strove with us to make us know Him and believe in Him and obey Him, and He strove even harder with the Father in order to obtain from Him pardon for us and the grace to believe in Him. During all that time He had gathered round Him only twelve apostles out of the entire population of the world.

Well then, how did He save mankind? How did He redeem the world? Today is the day of the Lord, the day when He comes to men. It is like that other great day. Then God came to unite Himself with man. Today God comes to man not in the hypostatic union, but to animate and regenerate him. Blessed day! Who can help marveling at it! Today light descends upon men, today the person of God Himself, the Holy Spirit, comes down and enters men's hearts.

Today is a day of great beauty and this union is indeed blessed! Today God saves the world through the Holy Spirit. "Then, why is Jesus Christ called the Savior?" The reason is that the Holy Spirit came to men through Christ's intercession, to heal their evil hearts, so inclined to wickedness. God complained through the mouth of Jeremiah: *Numquid servus est Israel, aut vernaculus? Quare ergo factus est in pracdam? Quare leones rugierunt super eum?*[18] Art thou a slave? Why then art thou become a prey to sin? Why have you let yourself be captured by the demon? Why are you, a Christian, now a slave? Why did you permit "the lions to roar upon him," to rejoice over him like vultures over dead bodies? Why did you allow him to be ground in the crushing-mill? Tell me: Why am I in sin, a slave to the devil? Raise your eyes to heaven, as Nebuchadnezzar did after seven years and say, as he did: "Lord, Thine is the kingdom and Thou wilt do according to Thy will."[19] In this way, I will teach you wisdom.

Thine is the power; health is in Thy hand. And if you have been wicked and mad and if your heart is overwhelmed, if you are aware of its weakness and obduracy, if it is fatigued and is suffering greatly, then the cure is at hand. God is telling you that you are soon to lose that beast's heart which you possess. May the Holy Spirit come and take from you that cruel, hard heart and give you a healthy heart in its place. As He cures what is within, He will also cure the exterior. When the priests entered the water, bearing the ark, they stopped running. When good thoughts (typified by the priests, because they offer us to God) enter the soul, they bring with them grace, which is the ark, and then all vice and wickedness cease, and men are changed. The Holy Spirit begins to accomplish His work. Man says: "Never again! I have offended my God up to now. That is enough!" Is this sufficient to prevent us from being wicked, from sinning? The philosophers Socrates, Plato, Pythagoras had all this. A virtuous man whose life is ruled solely by reason will not enter heaven, because only those who are born again can enter there. Men will not enter heaven unless they be children of God, full of faith, grace, hope, obedience. If you are guided by reason only, you will not enter there, for man's salvation must come from heaven. You will not be born again, even if you have been granted the strength to do good works, for even this path will not lead to salvation. You are not safe if you have not the habits of the virtues. You must possess within you a love that moves you. You must be infused with faith and charity, but this is not enough. Even if you are in health, without God's help there is no true health. May God bestow upon you those virtues which the theologians call habits. They are like the bracelets and jewels which are placed by way of adornment on a bride, though she is beautiful without them. St. Jerome says that "the riches of the Old Law prefigured the greatness which was to be given in the Law of grace."[20] Thus God enriches the powers of the soul, to make them function more effectively. It is not enough for the Holy Spirit that your outward demeanor be admirable; He wants you to be beautiful within. Not only should your actions be pleasing to Him, but also the desires that prompt these actions. And if you could see the beauty which the Holy Spirit brings to the soul where He dwells, you would follow it enchanted, and all the beauties of this world would fill you with disgust. When He who created the sun is in your soul, what must it be like? The bride of the Holy Spirit should be thus. As the spouse says in the Song of Songs: *Quam pulchra es, amica mea, quam pulchra es!*[21]

Attend to what I say. Who is so powerful that He can give you such love for the Holy Spirit that you will gladly follow Him! Since you say, when these gifts are in your soul, that the Holy Spirit is within you, why does St. John say: "for as yet the Spirit was not given, because Jesus was not yet glorified?"[22]

Listen: You have seen a master remove a pupil from his school when he knows as much as he himself does. He says to him: "Go and practice the science you have learned. Now you are a good doctor. Go and heal the sick!" The pupil leaves his master and works on his own account. That is what I have told you to do up till now. The Holy Spirit gives you faith and charity and innumerable virtues, and leaves you to accomplish the rest. As when a doctor says to a man whom he has cured: "Now you can eat everything, you are quite well. Live like a healthy man." "Since you have been educated, live accordingly." That is the moment when the Lord comes to your soul and enables you to behave as you ought, enlightens your understanding, directs your will, inflames you with the love of God, and gives you strength to love Him.

"But why must I do still more?" That is the point. St. Thomas expressed this better than anybody. He took it from St. Augustine, or rather, from Jesus Christ.[23] He says that all the graces and virtues that have been given you are not sufficient to save you, unless the hand of the Lord rests upon you in all your actions. Not that you cannot love God and believe in Him if you are in possession of these gifts, but to derive full benefit from them, the hand of the Lord must always be upon you. Without it, you cannot avail yourself properly of His presents. *Qui ex Deo est non peccat.*[24] You will be asked: "Why does he sin who is in the state of grace, since he has this strength, this help?" Because we have free will. Although you may possess many graces, you may cease to act in accordance with them, and you may fall into sin on this account. So that you may always avail yourself of them, the hand of the Spirit touches your soul,—it does not touch the gift, for that is not necessary—it touches your free will so that you will not lose grace although you are still free, and so that you may remain always constant. That is what the Holy Spirit is for, to keep you from sinning, although you may sin, since you are free. The Holy Spirit is essential to us, for without Him no one, no matter how many graces he may have, can save himself. That is what David said: *Spiritus tuus deduces me in terram rectam.*[25] No matter how well equipped a sailing ship may be, no matter how many instruments she may carry, if there is no pilot to steer her, she will be lost. So, too, if you have not the Holy Spirit, no matter how many graces you have, you will be lost. Blessed be Thou, oh Lord, who were not content with giving us Thy Son who died, but also Thy Holy Spirit, to be our teacher.

"What is different? Did not the holy men of the Old Testament have the Holy Spirit?" "Yes, they did." But the difference is that in those times, He gave Himself in small measure, and therefore did not affect them very deeply. But after the Holy Spirit came, He directed the apostles at every step and in nearly everything they did.

Today is the feast of the Holy Spirit. Now listen carefully! It is one thing to do good from merely human motives; it is quite another matter if the Holy Spirit is the author and mover of these actions and man hardly anything more than an instrument. It is very praiseworthy to perform a good work, if you deliberately make an effort and choose to do it, influenced by your virtue and good habits. It is, however, quite different to do some great deed without having planned it in advance or chosen to do it, if in fact, in the normal course of events, you had neither the strength nor the virtue to carry it out, and if neither ordinary faith or charity would suffice to make you do it, you have performed a deed as a young child speaks: his words being prompted by another. It is as if a great painter held the hand of one who did not know how to paint, and with it, painted a very beautiful picture. We say that he who holds the man's hand is the painter, but his instrument is the hand of the other. So it is here. When man performs a deed with the help of his own virtue and with the help of God, man is acting helped by God. When God is with him, the man is, as it were, the instrument of the Holy Spirit, so that if you asked him: "Who told you to do that? When did you think about doing that? Why did you do it?" he would be unable to give the reason. He only knows the deed has been done. The Holy Spirit is like a wind of which none can say from whence it comes or whither it goes. The Holy Spirit moves you. What great deed you performed which was far beyond your strength and which you are amazed to have accomplished!

I will tell you. How often have you longed to have devotion and it has come to you in small measure, because it is given in proportion to the sanctity of your soul? Has it not happened on other occasions, when your mind was occupied elsewhere, that a tremendous fire of love came to you and set your heart and soul aflame and you said: "I never expected such a thing to happen?" That came about not through any merit of yours, nor through effort nor virtue. Well, what was the cause? This is the feast of the Holy Spirit. As God, He moved you to do something for which your own strength was not sufficient. When something of the kind takes place within you, and you say: "I never expected to receive the Holy Spirit," this means that the Holy Spirit dwells within you. When you have true contrition you want to cry: *Abba, Father!* [26] Be careful never to act unworthily, but stay always near to God. The Holy Spirit gives Himself to us to help us in this and in other ways.

Notes

1. Dt 30:11–14.
2. Rom 10:6–8.
3. Dn 7:10.
4. Heb 9:24.
5. Heb 1:3.
6. Jn 3:17.
7. Jn 3:3ff.
8. St. Augustine, *In Io*. Ev., tr. 2, 6; tr. 7, 5: ML 35, 1478, 1486.
9. Nm 21:6–9.
10. Jn 3:16.
11. Ps 48:21.
12. Dn 4:13.
13. Job 6:7.
14. St. Augustine. *Serm*. 156 e. 2: ML 38, 850.
15. Rom 5:20.
16. Jn 3:17.

17. Ez 11:19; 36:26.

18. Jer 2:14–15

19. Dn 4:31–32.

20. St. Jerome; *Comm. in Eecl.* ML 23, 1079, 1081; cf. In Job. c. 42: ML 26, 848.

21. Song 4:1.

22. Jn 7:39.

23. St. Thomas, *Summa*, 1–2 q. 109, a 9., St. Augustine *Do nature et gratia*, c. 26; ML 44, 261.

24. 1 Jn 3:6; 5:18.

25. Cf. Ps 142:10.

26. Rom 8:15; Gal. 4:6.

Sermon VI

Ego vend ut vitam habeant, et abundantius hebeant. I am come that they may have life and may have it more abundantly (John 10:10).

■ ■ ■

Affairs in which life is involved are considered to be of the utmost importance and are conducted with the greatest care and attention. When we say: "Oh Lord, the safety of my life depends on this!" everything comes to a standstill.

We read that in former times our Lord gave a son to a good woman in response to the prayers and pleadings of the prophet Elisha. One day, going out to the fields the boy died: a severe headache had made him return home and he died in his mother's arms. The good woman placed his dead body on the prophet's bed and, in deep distress, went to Mount Carmel in search of Elisha. Throwing herself at his feet in bitterness and anguish of heart, she said: "Man of God! *Numquid petivi filium a Domino meo? Numquid non dixi tibi . . .* [1] The pain I have suffered at his death is greater by far than my joy and happiness when he was born." Then the prophet told his servant to take his staff and go to the dead child and touch his body with it. But the woman was not satisfied with this; again she threw herself at his feet and said: "As the Lord liveth and as thy soul liveth I will not leave thee unless thou dost accompany me."[2] The woman's importunity was such that the prophet went with her to her house. Approaching the bed where the child lay dead, he bent his body over that of the dead child, put his mouth upon his mouth, and his eyes upon his eyes and his hands upon his hands and his body upon his body. Finally, he lay altogether upon the child, contracting his body, and he who was dead became alive, he who had expired returned to life. The prophet took the boy and gave him alive to his mother saying: "Take up thy son."[3] Is there a mother here who has wept at the death of a child? Is she to learn to pray to and importune some holy prophet?

The Holy Spirit has been called *Seed,* because, just as you are born in the natural life through blood, so in the supernatural life the Holy Spirit takes the place of blood. The same love that comes through blood relationship is given by the Holy Spirit to the soul where He dwells and to which He comes. Understand that if the Holy Spirit comes to you, you will love your neighbors as much as you do your own brothers, and even more than your brothers. "Why?" Because the bond, the link generated in you by the Holy Spirit, is stronger than the ties of blood which make people love only father, mother, brothers, and relations.

The holy Virgin Mary had only one son, Jesus Christ, our Redeemer, and He was the child of her body; but because the Holy Spirit was infused into her heart and soul in abundance, she loves us greatly, she loves us deeply. There is no comparison between the love of a husband for his wife, of a mother for her child, of a child for its father and the spiritual love Mary feels for us as her adopted children. "What is the reason for this?" The Holy Spirit Himself is tenderness, is love. *Deus caritas est.*[4] And as such great abundance and plenitude of love was given to the Virgin, the child's mother cannot be compared to her. The prayers, supplication, and tears of our true Mother caused Him who is great to become small, Him who is above all things to become a creature, to humble Himself, to bend down and abase Himself, Him who is eternal to make Himself mortal. It is through the prayers of this Lady that everything we ask for will be granted to us by the Lord.

"I am come that they may have life and have it more abundantly."[5] This gospel is directed to shepherds. Since there are none here we will adapt it to suit ourselves who are the sheep.

You know that God, Our Lord, loves us. This love is very ancient. We do not cast off an old friend. You know that everything created by Our Lord God was for us, for our use and benefit. He created the sky and the earth, the sun and the moon, the sea and all that lives within it, the stars, the trees, the fishes, the animals. Lord, my God, for what purpose? For man's benefit and pleasure: "I want to prepare a house for my child." The universe had been created, but the house was empty. He created man out of the vilest slime of the earth, and like a good potter, after He had formed him out of earth, He *breathed into his face the breath of life* (the Hebrew says *through his nostrils*).[6] After receiving the breath of the Lord, man stood up alive.

Sicut corpus sine spiritu mortuum est . . . [7] Just as the body that cannot breathe is dead, so the soul is dead that has not the Holy Spirit. This Holy Spirit is the spirit of our soul. God, Our Lord, breathed into the first man *spiraculum vitae, the breath of life,* and then man became alive. That was a figure of the life of the spirit. Our Lord God gave Adam a body, and so that his body might have life and live, He gave it a soul to animate it. So that the soul also might have life, He gave it the Holy Spirit, *Spiritus vitae,* says St. Paul;[8] life of my life, soul of my soul. God breathed into man bodily life and also spiritual life. He gave him the Holy Spirit.

Did you never consider how our first parents, though living these two lives (the life of the body and the life of the soul) ate the apple and died, for their sin cost them their lives? How fitting that was. The entire happiness of a creature who wishes to please God consists in renouncing his liberty, his own will, his own wishes. Eve walked through the garden. The devil deceived her by advising her to eat of a certain tree. She ate of the tree and her soul died, because sin to the soul is like pestilence or arsenic to the body. *Jut potest aliquis gustare, quod gustatum affert mortem?*[9] "Who among you is" so out of his senses "that he would eat a dish" knowing for certain "that if he eats it, it will kill him?" Our first parents were told they must not eat of the forbidden tree, and Our Lord informed them that if they ate of it they would die. They ate of that tree and they died. To provide food for their bodies, God had put a great number of trees in this earthly paradise; for their spiritual food He had ordered them not to eat of the tree of life. He exacted this obedience from them for the good of their souls. Our first parents ate of the trees in paradise which Our Lord had created for them. They led spiritual lives, and were happy. By refraining from eating of the forbidden tree, they ate the fruit of obedience and led spiritual lives. Then they disobeyed the commandment which God Our Lord had given them, and their souls suffered death, through their disobedience. Because they insisted on doing what they wanted, their souls died. They were condemned to die in the body. Whether you like it or not, it is your fate to die in the body. Consider yourselves dead, even now, for life is nothing but a long drawn-out death. You are like a man in prison who has been sentenced to be hanged and who knows there can be no appeal from his sentence and that there is no hope. You consider that man dead, since he is so near death and since nothing can save him. Our father Adam died in the soul and died in the body, and all of us who descended from him are obliged to die as he did.

What is the remedy? Who can save us from this death of body and soul? The Gospel tells us. Our Lord Jesus Christ says: *Omnes quotquot venerunt, fures sunt.*[10] "All others, as many as have come before Me, are thieves and robbers."

In what state did the human race find itself? In what state were we? The soul was dead and we were condemned to die in the body. In what state is a man who has lost grace? He is like a man who has been condemned to death, and whose body after death will be used for experiments in dissection. He will be divided in pieces and cut up limb by limb. That can be done to him because he is dead. What cruelties the devil and his followers perpetrate on the soul that has lost God, that is dead through sin! How they ill-treat him! How they cut up that man who has lost his soul, who has been condemned to death because he offended God our Lord. Please God we shall never experience that! But if you do experience it, when temptation comes you will be cut in pieces; when a carnal pleasure is set before you, you will succumb at once; when the flesh yields the devil will ill-treat you and the world will do the same. All strike the soul that abandons God, that turns away from God through sin. Everyone wounds it and slashes it and cuts it in pieces. They stab you because you refused to pardon an injury; they stab you again for bearing a grudge against someone; and yet again to bring it home to you that you stole from your neighbor. *All are robbers as many as are come before me;* all those that come to your soul are robbers: *fures sunt.*

The lawyers call a robber one who robs in the daytime, in the daylight. A temptation of the flesh came to you, and although you knew that in consenting to commit that sin you would without any doubt lose God: although you understood and believed that that sin would deprive you of God and of His friendship: you committed it notwithstanding. This thought, this temptation, is the robber who comes in the daytime, who attacks in the daylight, since he persuades you to consent to sin, though you know you are doing wrong, though you know that through that sin you will lose God and His friendship and His grace. Your blindness and your misfortune are indeed great, since you realize what a misfortune it is to be deprived of God, since you realize that all you will gain will be hell for all eternity.

You are ready to lose God for a despicable pleasure that will pass in a moment. An evil, ugly deed is of more importance in your eyes, than God. With your eyes open you choose evil and reject God, the source and fathomless origin of all good. When you do this, you cease to exert yourself—though this is not quite accurate since you freely choose to act. This choice of yours is the robber who comes by day and robs you of your soul, deprives it of God and leaves it full of evil of every kind.

The thief who comes by night is more dangerous, is more to be feared. A noble thought comes to you and God inspires you with the wish to act upon it. You say to yourself: "Why do I want riches? Why do I want luxury? Why do I want empty honors? I will give all that up. I will do with very little. I want to be poor. I do not want to lead a social life. I do not want a life of trickery. I do not want high office. I do not want any of the rewards of this world." Then someone comes to you and says: "Give up these ideas! You are aiming at perfection. That is a life for those who are perfect. Of course you can carry on your business and go about in society and be rich and still save your soul. Who can stop you from serving God, from giving alms and doing a great deal of good, even though you are rich. Riches, on the contrary, will equip a man better to save his soul than poverty. For poverty brings with it many evils and distracts a man by making him worry over the necessities of life which more often than not he is without. Come now, this is not what God wants. He likes to see those who serve Him smiling and happy. To be sad, to go about looking downcast, to wear torn, cheap clothes will mark you out, people will say you are a saint, and you will fall into the sin of pride. It would be much better if you behaved like everybody else and were not remarkable in any way; if you were friendly with everyone and dressed reasonably well. It is better to be humble of heart than to give the impression of humility in your outward appearance, for God looks at the heart. A pious exterior does not interest Him; it tends to hide the sanctity of the heart. If you behave as I advise you to, you will be more secure." All this comes from the devil. He does not, of course, intend that you should stop at this point, because to behave thus is not evil in itself. He wishes to lead you gradually from here into a position of danger, where you will be separated from God. Therefore he would like to give you to understand that there is no danger, where on the contrary danger exists. These advisers are the thieves who come disguised as upright, reasonable men.

But there are other and greater dangers than these that will do even greater damage. May God preserve us from souls that are in the image of beasts, that are lower than brute animals: *Homo cum in honore esset non intellexit, comparatus est iumentis insipientibus, et similis factus est illis.*[11] "And man when he was in honor"—for God created him thus—"did not understand" what he had; he sinned, and "he is compared to senseless beasts, and is become like to them." But what will God Our Lord say when He sees that a worm of a man, an insignificant creature whom He knows to be despicable and ungrateful is full of pride? You said that you were rich and you are poor; you said you were good and you are evil. May God keep you, for your sake, from the least pride of heart; may God keep you, brother, from the least presumption, from the least vainglory. A Christian! Proud of what? The prouder we are the more ashamed and abashed we should be, the more we should despise ourselves. We live like animals, we eat like animals, we sleep like animals, and we die like animals.

God had compassion on us; because He created us, He would never cease to help us. And what, if you please, did this help cost? Eve committed one sin. It proved very costly. Jesus Christ, the Second Person of the Blessed Trinity, and the Holy Spirit, came to this world to save you from this disaster. Think about your belief that the Son of God and the Holy Spirit came to this earth to rescue you. Since the soul of man is like God in its *nature,* in its *goodness,* and in the *knowledge* it has of God, the *being* of the soul was not destroyed; although man dies, the soul will not die. It will live for ever. As the Father is the source of the Divine persons, He is considered to be the absolute being; and as man's immortal being was not lost, the Father did not come. Man lost his *knowledge* of God and the Son came; man lost his *goodness* and the Holy Spirit came.

The Son came so that our sins might be forgiven. The Son came because He was exceedingly angry with our first parents who had eaten the apple so that they might have the *wisdom* of the Son; and because as St. Paul says, "we were children of wrath."[12] God did not consider us as His children, but as wicked slaves. In the eyes of the Father, we were detestable. Jesus Christ came to the world so that through His coming for love of men, the Father might love men and look on them favorably and dwell among them.

That was Jesus Christ's mission: He wanted His Father, who had abandoned man on account of his sin, to look kindly on him again for His son's sake. If you see the Child weep at the door of His home and in the crib, this is the reason He is crying. If you see Him circumcised, this is why He was circumcised. If you see Him suffer hunger, it is for this He suffers hunger. If you see Him thirst, it is for this. If you see Him bound to a pillar and flogged, it is for this. If you see Him buffeted and crowned with thorns, it is for this. If you see Him nailed to a Cross, it is for this. His love for us knew no bounds.

Oh, my Redeemer! What moved Thee to suffer so much for love of men? What merchandise, Lord, dost thou go in quest of with such eagerness, that neither the heat of the sun by day nor the night-frosts deter Thee? Heavenly merchant, what dost Thou search for even though Thou art so very tired? We are told that Jacob served his father-in-law Laban for fourteen years so that he might receive Rachel as his wife, and during that time he slept out of doors in the cold and the heat, and thought little of the hardships he had undergone.[13] All love is insignificant in comparison with the love of Jesus Christ. All love is cold beside His love. Oh, my Redeemer! Didst Thou not work for Rachel? Jesus Christ worked and labored in this world for another Rachel, not for fourteen, but for thirty-three years and during all that time never rested a single day. Oh, blessed be He who loved so much! Jesus Christ walked by day and by night, in the cold and the wind, in the heat of summer. What hardships, what sufferings, our Redeemer underwent for the sake of His Spouse! How many nights didst Thou spend, oh my Redeemer, without sleep, weeping for us, praying and beseeching Thy eternal Father to pardon mankind. The apostle St. Paul said: *In diebus carnis suae preces suplicationesque ad eum, qui possit ilium salvum facere a morte . . .* [14] "Who, in the days of his flesh" all the time He lived in this world, "was offering up prayers and supplications" to His Father to save us for He alone was able to save us. Oh, who would not wish to have been able to come across Him, when he was weeping alone and say to Him: "My Redeemer, why art Thou weeping? What is wrong? Who is the cause of these tears? Who would be worthy to wipe them away?" Jesus Christ wept so that you might be happy; wept so that you might have peace; wept so that you might be consoled; wept on earth so that you might go to heaven; wept that your sins might be pardoned and that you might draw near to Him and that you might never offend Him.

What is it, Lord, that Thou seekest so anxiously? He Himself tells us: "Father, I seek nothing, nor do I wish for anything except that Thou shouldst love men with the same love as Thou hast for Me." It is as if He said: "I know, my Father, that Thou wilt love them now on My account. I want to be within them, so that in loving Me, Thou wilt also love them." Our Redeemer spent His whole life working for our happiness. He experienced fatigue and suffering, mental as well as physical, but hardship and pain were to Him of little account in comparison with His desire for our redemption. He wanted to save us, cost what it might. He Himself said it: "Why do you think I came into the world but to cast fire on the earth? And what will I, but that it be kindled? And I have a baptism wherewith I am to be baptized. And how am I straitened until it be accomplished?"[15] He was the fire and He had to be set alight. Our Redeemer knew that for Him baptism meant the shedding of His blood on the Cross and He longed for this to be accomplished. Lord, may the angels bless Thee for it! He is not like us who, at the approach of even the slightest hardship, imagine that we will be overwhelmed, and fly from it with all speed. He knew that it would cost Him a great deal if His Father were to love men again, but notwithstanding, He was ready to make the sacrifice. He knew that He would be scorched with the fire of suffering on the Cross and He said: "I long for the fire to be kindled." Our Savior had to be burnt on the Cross as a lamb was burnt in sacrifice in the Old Law. "Suffering is unimportant to Me; I am longing for the day when I can help man." *Qui proposito sibi gaudio, sustinuit crucem confussione contempta,* says St. Paul; "Having joy set before him, endured the cross willingly, despising the shame."[16]

"Lord, what makes Thee joyful? My Redeemer, what is the cause of Thy joy?" The Redeemer was happy because the human race was freed from sin, though He realized what the remedy would cost which was to cure us. He well knew—may the angels bless Him—that He would have to be branded so that we might have health. Do you know how? Have you not seen men walk the roads in the sun and the wind, thirsty and sweating, so that their children will be rich one day? They do not mind how hard they work and gladly suffer hardship and fatigue. Have you not seen a mother, who in her efforts to relieve her daughter's sufferings, rests neither night nor day and is utterly oblivious of her own comfort. In the same way our Redeemer, Jesus Christ—may He be blessed!—did not feel His sufferings greatly, and if He was keenly aware of them, the thought that through them we should be freed, made Him ignore them and think only of the universal good which would result from them. "All this is nothing," He said.

Blessed be Thou, my Lord, who said: "Let them give me five thousand blows!" so that a certain soul might be chaste. The thought of us all was in His heart, source of charity and love. "So that that other soul may be charitable, let them be uncharitable towards Me! So that this soul may be saved and all men obtain pardon, let them raise Me on a cross crowned with thorns, let them crucify Me, and let not a drop of blood in My whole body be unshed! Let them give me gall and vinegar to drink, and let me die on a cross!" "Why?" "To save mankind."

The Christian, who is redeemed by these sufferings, should learn not to feel dismayed by any little trial that may come to him. The moment a trial appears, you complain and say it is quite unbearable. Since Jesus Christ suffered so much, learn of Him; and since He turned His thoughts to saving you and disregarded the dreadful torments He had to undergo, you should, for His sake, ignore any trials that may come to you and fix your eyes on Jesus Christ. As you look at Him for whose sake you are suffering, pray that these trials may never cease and they will seem to you sweeter than honey.

So much was won for us by Jesus Christ through His agony, so great the grace He obtained for us from His Father, that now no man can offend God, if he chooses to avail himself of Christ's remedy. What a heroic deed it was to obtain pardon for all mankind! What a loving kiss of peace! What a sweet and loving embrace! If you want to repent you must not lose the remedy that will cure you and for which Jesus Christ paid in full. He himself wants you to approach Him, because what was lost has been regained. Now Jesus Christ has put an end to our sickness; now He has completed His task. He Himself said: "Father, forgive them!"[17] Look on them with favorable eyes. "Now, Father, I have finished the work which thou gavest me to do." *Opus consummavi quod dedisti mihi, ut faciam.*[18] "The work which thou gavest me to do is finished;" the deliverance of man is accomplished. Brethren, by this remedy the understanding was cured, the will was cured, the flesh was cured, all our sins were atoned for.

"Father, what remedy was given today?" It is this day which saw the end of the Law given so long before. Today a new Law and a better was given. The Old Law was written on tablets of stone, but this law was written on men's hearts. *Dabo legem mean in visceribus eorum.* "I will give my Law," said God through Jeremiah, "in their bowels."[19] It will not be written on paper or stone, but in their hearts, and it will bestow upon them chastity, humility, fortitude, and all the other virtues." The old Law was given on a mountain—on Mount Sinai. The new Law was given on the Mount of Sion. The old Law descended upon a high mountain and the new law also. But there was a difference. *Sion* means *watchtower,* because, some say, there was a tower in that place built by David which surpassed Jerusalem. *Watchtower,* giving man to understand that those who wish to receive the Holy Spirit must be alert and vigilant. They must not be preoccupied with other matters, but should be thinking of the arrival of the Holy Spirit. Their minds should not dwell on evil, nor should they be concerned with the things of this world, with wickedness, sin, or infamy. Their thoughts should be of God. Their hearts should not be soiled with abominations, but should be raised to Jesus Christ in faith, because the Holy Spirit is given through Him; He comes through His merits. Have faith in Jesus Christ!

The old Law was given on Mount Sinai and it ordered this to be done and not that. With the new Law is given the power to fulfill everything that was commanded by the old Law. I do not know if you understand me. I think not. Before God gave the Law on the mountain, lightning and thunder and the sound of trumpets caused great amazement and terror among the people. The whole mountain shook and all those who saw the sight trembled. They were all so terrified that they said to Moses: "Speak thou to us: let not the Lord speak to us."[20] God gave them commandments which filled them with fear. Because when a man looks into his heart and finds that he has not kept the Law, he discovers there a thousand misdeeds, a thousand defects. You cannot observe the Law which was given to you, since the Law is of heaven and you are of earth. That law caused terror, like the fire on the mountain where God appeared amid thunder and lightning. And what took place the day the Law was given on Mount Sinai was a figure of the Law that was to be given on Mount Sion. The old Law made people afraid. "How shall I be able to keep it?" But the new Law of today gives strength to keep the Law. If a man is unable to be chaste, this new Law will give him the strength to be chaste. If he cannot be humble this Law will give him the strength to be humble. If he cannot resist desiring the wife of another, this Law will give him the grace not to have this desire. In a word, it gives a man the strength, the power, the grace to obey the Law. Faced with the old Law, men were weak and terrified. The Law seemed to them harsh in the extreme because those who broke it were consigned to hell. The apostle St. Paul considering this matter and realizing how subject man was to the law of the flesh, said: *Infelix ego homo! Quis liberabit me a corpore mortis huius?* He called out: "Unhappy man that I am! Who shall deliver me from the body of this death?"[21] realizing he was so slow to obey the law and so prone to break it. But the new Law, when it came, gave strength to all men and helped them to obey the Law.

The Law which was given on this day, is the Law of the gospel. "Of which gospel? Of these Gospels which were written down?" No, because this Gospel is not properly speaking a gospel, but is merely called a gospel. The holy evangelical law is that law which is imprinted in men's hearts and which, although it is not written with letters, is capable of being clearly understood and of being obeyed. When this law was given to men, they received at the same time the desire to obey it. It was not necessary to say to men, "Be chaste!" for they were given the desire to be chaste. It was not necessary to tell men they must not be lustful, for when they had received the Law, their flesh was mortified as Jacob's flesh had been mortified, when the angel injured the muscle of his thigh.[22] The Law did not order them to be patient, but bestowed on them kindness, love, and goodwill, and the power to endure adversities of all kinds. All this is not conveyed by word, nor revealed to the intellect. *Vos estis Epistola mea.*[23] It is not necessary to write an epistle in order to transmit the Law. "You," says the apostle St. Paul, "are our Epistle, your hearts are the letter. Do not imagine the Law must be written in ink. It is written with the finger, by the Holy Spirit. He wrote the Law in your hearts which I preached to you. The Holy Spirit wrote it," says St. Paul; "and it is promulgated through me." This Law gives charity and humanity and all the other virtues too; and because it can be understood even by old women, this Law makes saints, makes men just and gives grace.

Today we celebrate the occasion when God gave grace to the world. The old Law was given on a mountain, and by the new Law grace was given to us on a mountain. There was the sound of trumpets then as now. But if men were terrified in those days, now they are merely a little timid. It is as if you were to be awakened at midnight when everything is quiet, peaceful, tranquil, by the sound of sweet harmonious music. For a moment you are somewhat nervous, and then your fear vanishes. You feel a breath of wind—it has come to warn you, as if to tell you to listen attentively.

"What day is today?" "The day of consolation." "What day is today?" "Today the Paraclete came from heaven to earth." "What day is it today, Father?" Today is a feast of such importance and significance that he who does not participate in it, will not participate in the graces of any other feast of Jesus Christ. Though Jesus Christ's death gained pardon for sin, it would be of no benefit to you without the grace which is given today. Listen carefully! What will it profit you to spend your entire fortune on a highly efficacious remedy, if after buying it, you decide not to take it? How can a medicine cure your illness, if you refuse to take it? You will continue to be ill and you will be obliged to pay for the medicine. All that Jesus Christ underwent, His death and sufferings, were the remedy He obtained for your illness. If you decide to take it you will be cured, you will be freed from all guilt. If you refuse to take it, you will pay in hell for all that Jesus Christ suffered. If you accept it, Jesus Christ will be pleased indeed and will consider Himself well rewarded for all that He went through in this world. But if you do not wish to participate in today's feast, if you do not wish to receive the Holy Spirit, *si quis non habet Spiritum Christi, hic non est ejus.*[24] "If any man have not the Spirit of Christ, he is none of His!" He cannot be saved.

Today is the *seventh day* of Jesus Christ's work. Today *he breathed into the face of man* to give him life. After His life, His holy incarnation, His death, His resurrection, on the day of His holy ascension He accomplished all that was necessary so that man might have life. This is the day when He breathed into the heap of earth. And if at the time of creation He breathed into the earth a soul for the body that as yet had no life, today He breathes into man the life of grace. Because if man's soul is without grace, it is dead. And if grace comes to the soul and gives it life, it is because today God breathed into the heap of earth.

"What was that heap of earth, Father?" "Christ's apostles." And of what earth they were! One day, before Jesus Christ went to heaven He told them He would send them a Paraclete. They waited for Him day after day until Pentecost. It seemed to them that He was not going to come and they were dismayed. Their fervor had cooled and they were anxious; like the two who had gone away while the others were waiting for the Resurrection, they said: "Our Master has gone away. He told us He would send us a Paraclete; we have been expecting Him for a long time now and He has not come. We are without our Master, without anyone to console us. What are we to do? We are like sheep without a shepherd, frightened and discouraged."

But they were all sensible about one thing, that is, they did not want to go away from the world without taking leave of the most Blessed Virgin Mary. I consider it a great mystery that the Mother of God should have remained among the apostles after the passion as well as after the ascension. If a temptation of the flesh comes to you, if some evil man comes and tries to lead you astray, tries to make you defile your body and your soul, you have an advocate in the Virgin Mary. Say with confidence: "The Mother of God is the Mother of purity. She is immaculate. She has the power to intercede for me. I will not reject Jesus Christ without talking to His Mother first of all." You may take it as certain, brethren, that if you go to the Mother of God, if you commend yourself to her, you will receive consolation and relief for all the suffering you are undergoing.

Our Lord's apostles and disciples, and a number of good men to the number of about one hundred and twenty were in the Cenacle; at one end were the men and at the other the Virgin, Our Lady, the Marys and the other holy women. Being in great distress they said: "Let us speak to the Virgin, since she has been left to console us." They were feeling sad, downcast, and melancholy. They went to her and told her how miserable they felt and how their Master had delayed in coming to them; that they were among enemies and were unprotected. "Pray, Virgin, to your Son, to send us the Comforter He promised us," they besought her.

It was about nine o'clock in the morning, the hour when the Virgin used to go out to prayer. It was her custom to go out late, when the sun was already up, because this is a suitable hour for prayer. In fact from dawn until that hour, before men are busy with worldly interests and trivialities, is the best time to pray. The first hours of the day should be spent in the service of God. Our Lady, then, was praying and went out with a look of such peace and happiness on her countenance that at the sight of her those who were sad and afflicted felt consoled, the sick felt better and all who were frightened felt soothed. The most holy Virgin went to them as was her custom and gave them confidence, saying: "Why have you so little faith in your Master my Son? He will console you as He promised. Do you not know, beloved children and disciples of my most blessed Son, that the old Law was given more than fifty days after the Israelites left Egypt? It is now fifty days since my Son suffered death and led you out of the captivity of sin. The Holy Spirit will come today. Do you not know also that at the end of every fifty years the jubilee took place when prisoners were set free, and goods that were sold were given back to their owners; it was a year of festivity and great rejoicing, a year of forgiveness, when debts were remitted? So fifty days after the passion, the jubilee will take place, the Holy Spirit, the Paraclete will come and will free you from captivity. God will exempt you and not only you, but all mankind from the debt you owe Him; because it was decided that at the hour when God gave life to the body, when He gave it a soul, at that same hour He would give life to our souls. He will come at nine o'clock. Do not be anxious. Believe that He will come. Now sit down."

She made them all sit. They sat on seats, or knelt in prayer. She comforted them, restored their confidence; and then the most holy Virgin, having compassion on the little flock which remained with her, went down on her knees, raised her hands to heaven and with tears streaming from her blessed eyes, started to pray to her beloved Son: "Oh, my Lord and my sweet Son, I ask Thee through the love Thou hast for me, through the merits, of Thy blessed passion, deign to console Thy apostles. Send them, Lord, the Paraclete to console them. Lord keep the promise Thou didst make them in Thy name that the Holy Spirit, the Paraclete, would come. My Son, send Thy Holy Spirit to these weak men!"

It is indeed a wonderful sight to see that Mother pray to her Son; to see the Son pray, as man, to His Father. He Himself said it with His blessed mouth: "I will ask the Father and he shall give you another Paraclete. . . ." *The Lord had respect to Abel and to his offerings.*[25] Jesus Christ would appear as man before the Father, He would show

Him the marks of the nails, and His side pierced with a lance and He would say: "Father, have compassion on these lambs who are in the world without a shepherd; they are not strong, they are sad. Send them, Father, Thy spirit, for the sake of the sufferings which I underwent for their sake. They are waiting for the Paraclete I told them would be sent to them. Send Him to them, Father, for love of Me! *Non confundentur qui sperant in te, Domine.*[26] Let them never be confounded who have hoped in Thee, oh Lord! Do not let their hopes be in vain! Look, Father, at this Son, and do not refuse Him what He asks Thee; love them, My Father! They deserve to be consoled through My merits. Comfort them, Father, send them the Holy Spirit!" And you can be certain that He would make a very special petition to the Father to send the Holy Spirit. "Lord, do this also for the love of My mother who is waiting for Thee."

The Lord had respect to Abel and to his offerings. The bowels of the Father were moved with compassion by the prayers of His Son and for His sake He was heedful of the prayers of the most holy Virgin and of those little lambs. He looked favorably on all who were in that poor house, because of the merits of Jesus Christ which were great enough to pacify God's wrath which was directed against us. And observe that the Holy Spirit came to those men with the same love and with the same goodwill as if He were coming to Jesus Christ. Because after Christ died for us God looked at us with different eyes. He felt for us the same love as He had for His blessed Son.

The Holy Spirit came and the skies were opened; the veil of the Old Testament was torn and the *Sancta*

Sanctorum was visible. Now its doors were wide open; if anyone wanted to enter, he could do so. Before Christ died, a certain number of souls were saved; after His death the number was much greater. First of all a sound was heard which made the Cenacle tremble, so that they might realize that the Holy Spirit is strong. Then tongues of fire came and remained above the heads of those who were present, so that they might understand that the Holy Spirit is fire, that He is the ardor of the heart. When you feel as if there is a flame within you, that you heart is burning with the love of God, that is the Holy Spirit. This flame is a messenger upon whom you can rely, for the Holy Spirit is in the midst of it. The Holy Spirit, then, came to the apostles, embraced them, consoled them, gave them courage, gave them the kiss of peace.

"Father, tell us, what is the Holy Spirit like?" No tongue can describe, no ear can hear, no heart can feel what the kiss, the embrace of the Holy Spirit means. Elijah relates that God said to him: *Egredere, et sta in monte coram Domino. Et ecce Dominus transit, et spiritus grandis et fortis, subvertens montes, et conterens petras ante Dominum; non in spiritu Dominus; et post spiritum commotio, non in commotione Dominus; et post commotionem ignis, non tamen in igne Dominus; et statim venit sibilus tenuis aurae; illic Dominus.*[27] The Lord ordered Elijah to go to the mountain. Why? "Elijah, what didst thou see?" He answered: "There was a great wind" so strong that it overthrew the mountains, but "the Lord was not in the wind." After the wind ceased, what happened? "A fire, but the Lord was not there." After the fire there "came a whistling of a gentle air; the Lord was there."

What are you doing here, brother? Those to whom the Holy Spirit says: "What are you doing here? What are you doing, sinner, by this river that has gone dry, in this insalubrious place?" will very quickly leave it. When a man hears the voice of the Holy Spirit say to him: "What are you doing here?" he will immediately despise the world and care nothing for it. The Holy Spirit came in the whistling of a gentle air.

No one can tell you or describe to you what this embrace, this kiss of the Holy Spirit is like. The Holy Spirit is so good to him who possesses Him. *Qui adhaeret Domino, unus spiritus est cum eo.*[28] Be chaste! Oh, fortunate is he to whom the Holy Spirit comes. "He who is joined to the Lord is one spirit;" the Holy Spirit and he are one and the same.

"What is this, Father? Is it a marriage?" It is that of which Jesus Christ said: *Erunt duo in came una;*[29] "they two shall be in one flesh." "Why should God, who is the Holy Spirit, become one with man?" "To give man virtues to make him holy; to give him fine garments, to adorn and restore him to health. That is what the coming of the Holy Spirit, the embrace of the Holy Spirit, does to man. But that embrace cannot be described. A man gives jewels to his betrothed; He gives her bracelets for her arms, earrings for her ears. They are not yet married, but these gifts are a pledge of his intentions. That is what the Holy Spirit does. He gives the sinner jewels; puts the bracelets and bangles of the virtues and of good works on his arms, so that, thus sanctified, he may embrace Him. He also gives him earrings for his ears, asking him to listen attentively and obey the voice he hears within his heart. But this is not yet the marriage. He gives him His seven gifts. All these presents are a dowry, the coins the bridegroom gives his bride, and are presented to the soul to prepare it for the coming. They are the gifts of the bridegroom. But I do not know what the embrace means."

"Father, you said the Holy Spirit becomes one with that man in whom He dwells. Is that man then God? How wonderful that is." Does that surprise you? Then listen: *Ego dixi: dii estis, et filii excelsi omnes.*[30] God Himself said it. "I have said: you are gods." Do you know to what extent? That if a man has within him the Holy Spirit and speaks, the Holy Spirit is said to be speaking. "Do not be anxious or be solicitous concerning what you say," says Christ, *Non estis vos qui loquimni, sed Spiritus Patris vestri est qui loquitur in vobis.*[31]

St. Augustine said: "Without the Holy Spirit it is impossible to comprehend goodness and the supernatural. Goodness does not come from man alone."[32] When a man performs a good deed, it is not the work of man alone. He has a mother on earth and a father in heaven. Your free will is your mother, but not the more important of your parents; your other parent is more eminent, is greater, is the essence, is the father, the source of energy. Your other parent is the Holy Spirit. St. Paul says: "The Spirit himself asketh for us with unspeakable groanings."[33]

"Why?" "Because He is one with him who prays." "Then, if they are not two persons, there must be an incarnation." "Be careful! This only means that the Holy Spirit and he in whom He dwells are one; but they do not form one person, they are two persons." "But why?" "Because the Holy Spirit operates in man as the more important of the two. That is why it is said that such and such an action was performed by the Holy Spirit."

"But Father, you have not told us about the embrace. All you have said is beside the point." "No one can describe how that happened. It is true that the deeds and miracles performed by the apostles were inspired by the coming of the Holy Spirit. It is true that the Holy Spirit came to them; but the embrace He gave them . . . Forgive me!"

If all the perfumes in the world, among them civet, musk, amber, orange blossom, jasmine, were mingled together, without the smell of one being stronger than another, what a beautiful odor would result! How it would soothe you, how it would comfort your soul! Well, take note that, in comparison with the odor of the Holy Spirit, all these perfumes would seem more bitter, more disagreeable than gall. Oh what savor, what beauty of color, what a taste, what comfort, what peace, what joy, what happiness, what strength the apostles experienced when they felt within them the breath of the Holy Spirit! How happy, how satisfied, how contented they felt when their souls were filled to overflowing with the Holy Spirit! Beseech Him to give us the breath of the Holy Spirit, the "whistling of the gentle air."

What are we doing here, brethren? What is our business here? If we remain here, we cannot prosper. What are you doing here, sinner? How do you spend your time? This pool is dry, or in any event it will dry up soon. That fortune you relied on is gone, or it will soon go. You will be deprived of it; it will be taken from you. Why, unfortunate man, do you give your love to a woman, and why does she love you? This pool is dried up; you will die shortly, or she will, and you will find that the pool from which you hoped to satisfy your thirst is completely dried up. Why are you so proud and conceited? You will end badly. Everything will be taken from you. You drink now and when you least expect it, death will come to you. Woe to you, if you do not renounce the vanities and follies of this world! Since you place your trust in the things of the world, your eyes are not on heaven. Since you have not detached yourself from all that is here below, the Holy Spirit has not breathed upon you; you do not yet know the sweetness of God: *Quam magna multitudo dulcedinis tuae, Domine, quam abscondisti timentibus te!* "How great is the multitude of thy sweetness, O Lord, which thou hast hidden from them that fear thee."[34] Oh, may the earth and skies bless Thee! And if Thou hast provided so well for those that fear Thee, what wilt Thou do for those that love Thee? He is called brightness and fire.

Brother, do you know God? Tell me, has God united Himself to you? The chief sign by which you will know that God is with you, is that you will despise everything on earth that is not of God, and your one thought will be to love and please Him, as your only good. And you will know, brother, that the Holy Spirit has come to you if you walk along the path of Jesus Christ, filled with joy and fervor. If the Holy Spirit has said to you: "What are you doing?" all is well with you.

Oh, how did the apostles feel when the Spirit said to them: "What are you doing there?" There is no answer to that question, just as one cannot say who God is. What wonders He performed among them, what graces He gave them! He gave them the grace of understanding. Without these graces, what do learned men and the great philosophers amount to, and what do they know? Theologians who have not the grace of the Holy Spirit know nothing. The chief gift He gave the apostles was the understanding to know clearly how to behave in all human affairs, to be able to say with complete certainty: "This is the proper thing to do; that is not." We are all able to differentiate between good and evil in general terms but we are not always sure how to decide in individual cases. Without the Holy Spirit no one can know whether it is better for him to be married or unmarried, to be priest or layman, friar or not a friar. The Holy Spirit is the teacher of children. And how well instructed that child will be, who has learnt from such a Master!

Perhaps you may say: "It will not be necessary for a clever man to ask for advice as to what he should or should not do. He can be guided by his own judgment. He does not require advice from anyone." No, the Holy Spirit wishes everyone to seek advice from Him who knows more than you do. He will inspire you to do so; He will tell you what to ask and will give you the grace to respond as you should.

The Holy Spirit who gives understanding, who influences and guides the will, will not let you fall into temptations of the flesh. If it should occur to you to do something which is wrong, not only will He prevent you from doing it, but will make you do the opposite of what you had intended. If you are not convinced, consider the case of Jeremiah who, being ill-treated because he prophesied, said: "I am become a laughingstock all the day: all scoff at me. For I am speaking now this long time, crying out against iniquity: and the word of the Lord is made a reproach to me and a derision, all the day. Then I said: I will not make mention of him nor speak any more in his name."[35] At that moment fire came down from heaven and touched him, and had such an effect on him that where before he spoke one word, now he spoke four.

When fire comes down from heaven, when the Holy Spirit comes, He takes away man's fear, the fear of poverty, of dishonor, of hunger, of vituperation, death, temptations of the flesh, of the world, and of the devil. Man considers the worst consequences these things could have, a mere fleabite. *Quis nos separabit a caritate Christi?* says the apostle, St. Paul. *Tribulatio, an angustia, an fames, en nuditas, an periculum, an persecutio, an gladius?* "Who shall separate us from the love of Jesus Christ?" Who would be strong enough to deprive us of it? "Shall tribulation? Or distress? Or famine? Or nakedness? Or danger? Or persecution? Or the sword?"[36] None of these things can separate us from it, no matter how appalling they may seem to us; nothing can frighten us. All kinds of things may happen to us, but nothing can defeat us. In fact, the greater the misfortunes that assail us, the more will our love of Jesus Christ grow, so that we will be victorious wherever we may be, and over everything. We will be rich in virtue and honorable, not through our own strength, our own merits, but through the help and protection of Jesus Christ. Because, loving us, as He does, He will not allow us to be defeated. Nor will we be overcome by sin, for we will always be mindful of His graces and His marvelous works, of the favors we have received from Him, of how He delivered us from evil. Even when we tried to fall into the abyss of hell, His hand, His arm reached out to save us.

And if these perils, which are insignificant, seem to you to be formidable, wait and you will learn of far worse dangers. Invisible dangers that threaten the soul are a great deal more terrifying than those which harm only the body, for no matter how many or how severe they may be, they can do no more than kill us. But we are to fear none of them, because the apostle St. Paul himself says: "For I am sure that neither death, nor life, nor angels, nor principalities, nor powers, nor things present, nor things to come, nor might, nor height, nor depth," nor cruelty, nor misfortunes of the world, "nor any other creature shall be able to separate us from the love of God which is in Christ Jesus."[37]

"Did flesh or blood tell you that, Paul?" Neither. It was the Holy Spirit. He is the fire that burns and consumes all these things, as if they were straws, so that they will not injure us. In the presence of the fire of the Holy Spirit, they are no more than pieces of straw in an immense furnace. When you have the Holy Spirit within you, He will kill all that can harm you; but if some straws remain, it is evident that no fire has consumed them. If, brother, you are a slave to your vices, if you are inclined to evil, if you harbor unchaste thoughts in your heart, if you are proud, all that will be in the way of the Holy Spirit. The Holy Spirit, when He comes, will burn it all, and nothing will be able to resist Him. When the Holy Spirit comes, no one will be strong enough to withstand Him. Not the foolish young girl who spends her time thinking about her clothes, and how to make herself attractive, and what cosmetics to use on her face. When the Holy Spirit comes to her, this same young girl will take pleasure in dressing quietly; she will choose tears as a water to beautify her face; she will be humble. She will not be interested in the haughty young man who holds himself so straight, his sword by his side, with a feather in his cap. Do you know why they put that there? So that you may know, if you do not know it already, that they are mad, and so that you may be aware of their madness, their evil thoughts, their foolish ideas and their pride. However, when the Holy Spirit comes, He will burn it all.

Christ said: "Do not think I came to send peace on earth; I came not to send peace, but the sword."[38] Why is it that that young man who was so dissolute, so fond of gadding about, whose great amusement was to go through the streets after some girl, has lately begun to lead a retired life and is now chaste, humble and virtuous? Who brought about this change in him? The Holy Spirit. The fire that burns whatsoever comes in its way. Neither honors, nor riches, nor prosperity, nor any carnal pleasures that men may desire can exist together with this fire. It makes men despise these things and trample them underfoot. This fire burns away all man's sensuality. *Vivo ego, iam non ego.*[39] "And I live, now not I, but Christ liveth in me," says the apostle. I live in humility, in chastity, in patience. *Now not I:* not my former self, not my passions, my sensuality, because all that is now dead. "How did this happen, Apostle?" In what way? Jesus Christ lives in me through humility, through charity, through grace; and when this grace comes to man, it completely changes him, it makes him the reverse of what he used to be. He who formerly idolized himself, and had a high opinion of himself, now says: "May God be exalted, may I be humbled; may God be served, may I be despised; may God be honored, may I be dishonored; may God be glorified and may I be vilified!" He upon whom the Holy Spirit has breathed, desires nothing for himself, wants only God's honor and glory.

Before the Holy Spirit came to the apostles, they were fainthearted and timid and lived behind locked doors. They did not dare to go outside lest they should be killed. They were greatly afraid.

Once God brought the prophet Ezekiel in spirit to a plain where there was an infinite number of dead bones—a vast quantity of them and all exceedingly dry. And He said to Ezekiel: "Son of man, dost thou think these bones shall live?" Ezekiel answered: "Thou, Lord, knowest." God ordered him: *Vaticinare de ossibus istis.* "Prophesy concerning these bones." "How, Lord?" Say to them: "Ye dry bones, hear the word of the Lord. I will give you spirit and you shall live; I will lay sinews upon you and will cause flesh to grow over you and will cover you with skin and I will give you spirit and you shall live." "I," said Ezekiel, "prophesied as he had commanded me, and as I prophesied there was a noise, and, behold a commotion, and the bones came together, each one to its joint;" they made the noise of one bone joining with another. "And I saw, and behold the sinews and the flesh came upon them; and the skin was stretched out over them; but there was no spirit in them." They remained there as if they were dead. "Prophesy to the spirit, prophesy, and say to the spirit: Thus saith the Lord God: Come spirit, from the four winds and blow upon these slain and let them live again. And I prophesied as he had commanded: and the spirit came into them and they lived, and they stood up upon their feet, an exceeding great army. And God said: All these bones are the house of Israel. They say: Our bones are dried up and our hope is lost."[40]

The apostles were gathered there together, terrified, and as lifeless as dead bones. Are there any here who although they look as if they were alive, are, in reality, dead? Is there anyone here so lacking in hope that he says: "How can I be good? How is it possible for me to be chaste? How could God forgive me? I have sinned so frequently all my life that I have done nothing but offend God. How can He pardon me? Who am I to go to heaven? Who am I go to such a place? Heaven is given to those who perform good works; I have done no good works, nor do I even hope to do any. What concern have I with good works? Twenty times I have tried not to sin, and I have never been able to stop myself from sinning. *Iam aruerunt omnia ossa rostra, et periit spes rostra.* "Our bones are dried up and our hope is lost."

Oh, you are indeed unhappy if you talk thus! Make an effort, brother, because today is the day of forgiveness; today everyone will be accepted. All you have to do is acknowledge your sins, and be sorry for them and confess them. And you, young man, do you really think that you cannot avoid sin, that you cannot give it up? Try to renounce sin, for this is the day of forgiveness; today strength is given with which to overcome and overthrow that which has hitherto overthrown you; today you will be given the strength, if you want to receive it, to conquer your passions; today is the day when God promised to take away hearts of stone, to take away dryness of soul, today hearts are given that are tender and repentant; that are filled with the desire to bewail sins and to confess them. Today is the day when you will receive the breath of the Holy Spirit; it will not touch you externally, but you will feel it deep in your inmost hearts. This breath will give you life, will give you chastity, will give you humility, will give you charity and love and all the other virtues. This breath will refresh your souls.

If you do not believe me, look at the effects of the Holy Spirit on the apostles. They were all cowards because they were too wrapped up in themselves. But when the Holy Spirit came to them and entered their hearts, all fear left them; they spurned the flesh and renounced pride and envy; they cast off their vices trampling them underfoot, as victors tread upon those who once vanquished and terrified them and filled them with fear. "They stood up upon their feet, an exceeding great army." They opened the door which formerly they had kept shut. They were full to overflowing of the Holy Spirit, full of fortitude and charity, and they began to preach Christ's doctrine, not coldly and without ardor, but in words of fiery eloquence: "Blessed be God!" "There is but one God, three persons and one true God;" "Jesus Christ is the Son of the living God, and He is seated at the right hand of God, and is the Judge of the living and the dead." Thus they spoke, so that all might understand them.

People of all nations were gathered there together. There were Parthians, Medes, inhabitants of Mesopotamia, Judea and Cappodocia, of Asia Minor, of Phrygia, of Pamphilia, of Egypt, of Libya, of Crete, of Arabia, of Rome. All these people, though they spoke different languages, understood the apostles. Each one followed what was said, as if it were in his own language. Is this so strange since it is the work of God? Today, when a preacher speaks in the vernacular, each one hears the sermon in his own language; the preacher speaks as God commands, and he to whom his words are applicable, understands them. The rest do not comprehend him. One preacher says: "Be humble!" The proud man understands that. Another says: "Be chaste!" The libertine understands that. And so though the preacher speaks the same language to all, his words have a different meaning for each individual.

After the Holy Spirit had come, there was great excitement among all those who were gathered together in Jerusalem, because though the preaching was in one language, each man understood what was said in his own tongue, and they were astonished. "Are not all these that speak, Galileans? they asked, And how have we heard, every man our own tongue wherein we were born?" Others said: "These men are full of new wine."[41] When you do not understand what someone is saying to you, have patience and do not be quick to condemn him! Remember, the Holy Spirit is never seen. Someone may speak to you of what God wishes him to speak; be careful you do not say he is drunk!

For that is what they said of the apostles. Whereupon St. Peter, as universal pastor and as their defender, stood up and said: "Ye men of Judea, be this known to you. For these are not drunk as you suppose, seeing it is but the third hour of the day. But this is that which was spoken of by the prophet Joel:" *Effundam spiritum meum super omnem carnem, et prophetabunt filii vestri, et filiae vestrae.* "I will pour out," I will bestow "my spirit upon all flesh, and your sons and your daughters shall prophesy; and your young men shall see visions and your old men shall dream dreams. And upon my servants, indeed, and upon my handmaids will I pour out in those days of my spirit. Ye men of Israel, we preach of Jesus Christ, a man approved of God" whom you delivered up to death, with all the signs which God did by Him, whom God hath raised up, and He is at the right hand of the Father, "having loosed the sorrows of hell, as it was impossible that he should be holden by it. Therefore let all the house of Israel know most certainly that God hath made both Lord and Christ, this same Jesus, whom you have crucified."[42]

St. Peter preached with great fervor, telling them how the Holy Spirit longs to come and console and help us. The good fisherman throws out his net; he who used to catch fish is now a fisher of souls. At the first cast, St. Peter caught three thousand of those who, a short while previously, had said he was drunk. Full of compunction, they regretted what they had said. "We are indeed unfortunate," they declared. How can we become converted, for it was we who crucified Christ and asked for Barabbas to be set free? How can God pardon us? How is such a thing possible? Then St. Peter said to them: Why are you so upset?

Do not be discouraged! God is mercy and Jesus Christ is full of mercy. In spite of what you have done, in spite of the fact that you killed Him with your own hands, He will forgive you, if you repent and do penance. Confess your sins immediately, for the longer you delay in confessing them, the longer God will delay in pardoning you. When they heard this, they said they were willing to do as Peter said, and not only did God forgive them their sins, but was so merciful to them that He sent the Holy Spirit to them and to the apostles—nearly three thousand souls in all. You see what a good catch that was at the first throw! Oh, blessed be Thy mercy, my Lord! What cost you so dearly is now given away for nothing! God gave the Holy Spirit to whoever loved God, and asked for no payment.

At another sermon, five thousand men were converted. The number of Christians was increasing, and the Church of God, which had been so small, continued to grow larger and to gain more members. From that moment, Christianity, as we now know it, started. They all prayed together regularly; they communicated every day; sold all their possessions and gave the money to the apostles, saying: "This is the value of all my possessions. Take it and do with it what you will." All were equal and everything was held in common; he who contributed a small sum received as much as he who contributed a large amount. In the universal church of that time, as in monasteries today, no one had any possessions of his own, either for his private use or for use in common. This enabled them to be more detached. The holy apostles and the other pious men and women all lived in this manner.

They performed many miracles, many wonderful deeds; they cured the sick and made the dead to rise. Most of their time was spent in prayer and they were supremely happy for they were full of the Holy Spirit, and rejoiced in the presence of such a Guest.[43]

May the Holy Spirit, through the merits of Jesus Christ and the blood He shed for us on the Cross, deign to come to our hearts and cure our souls. May He enlighten our understanding so that we may come to know God. May He make us will to love only God, to renounce the things of the earth, and to mortify our flesh. May He give us humility, chastity, and charity towards our neighbors; may He give us His seven gifts, so that, having within us His grace, we may enter into glory with Him for ever.

Notes

1. 2 Kings 4:28.
2. 2 Kings 4:30.
3. Ibid. 36.
4. I Jn 4:16.
5. Jn 10:10.
6. Gn 2:7,
7. Jas 2:26.
8. Rom 8:2.
9. Job 6:6.
10. Jn 10:8.
11. Ps 48:13.

12. Eph 2:3.

13. Gn 29:18–30.

14. Heb 5:7.

15. Lk 12:49–50.

16. Heb 12:2.

17. Lk 23:34.

18. Jn 17:4.

19. Jer 31:33.

20. Ex 20:19.

21. Rom 7:24.

22. Gn 32:25.

23. 2 Cor 3:2.

24. Rom 8:9.

25. Jn 14:16; Gn 4:4.

26. Ps 21:6; 30:2.

27. 1 Kings 19:11–12.

28. 1 Cor 6:17.

29. Mk 10:8.

30. Ps 81:6.

31. Mt 10:20.

32. St. Augustine, Ep. 140, c. 35, 81; ML 33, 575; *Enarr. in Ps.* 126:4; ML 37, 1670; *Contra duas ep. Pelagianorum,* 1, 2, c. 9, 21: ML 44, 586.

33. Rom 8:26.

34. Ps 30:20.

35. Jer 20.

36. Rom 8:35.

37. Rom 8:38.

38. Mt 10:34.

39. Gal 11:20.

40. Ez 37:3–11.

41. Acts 2:7, 13.

42. Acts 2:14ff.; Jl 2:28ff.

43. Acts 2:42–47.

.